THE HAWAIIAN SENTENCE BOOK

By
Robert Lokomaikaʻiokalani
Snakenberg

Illustrated by
Robin Yoko Burningham

The Bess Press
P.O. Box 22388
Honolulu, HI 96823

Library of Congress
CATALOG CARD NO: 86-64041
 Honolulu, Hawaii: Bess Press
 112 pages — illustrations, Hawaiian Sentences, English Translations

Edited by LOKOMAIKA'IOKALANI SNAKENBERG and DR. ANN RAYSON
Designed by LOKOMAIKA'IOKALANI SNAKENBERG and PAULA NEWCOMB
Drawings on pages 3, 13, 21 and 90 by Kauanoelehua Chang

ISBN: 0-935848-44-4
Copyright © 1988 by The Bess Press
ALL RIGHTS RESERVED
Printed in the United States of America

TABLE OF CONTENTS

Foreword . . . . *iv*
Introduction . . . . *v*
About People 1
The Body 25
Hawaiian Lifestyles 29
Verbs & Adjectives 65
Clothing 81
Relative Locations 84
At School 88
English Translations of Hawaiian Sentences 94

FOREWORD

The *Hawaiian Sentence Book* was designed to answer the requests of many people in the community who bought and were delighted by the *Hawaiian Word Book,* which was first printed in 1982. That first book is an excellent resource for parents and grandparents to teach youngsters numerous useful and important Hawaiian terms. Teachers and *kūpuna* in the Hawaiian Studies program were also quick to incorporate the vocabulary from that book into their lessons.

The Bess Press was informed on many occasions that another book was needed to follow up on the Hawaiian language learning that was taking place among children and adults using the *Hawaiian Word Book.* This *Hawaiian Sentence Book* seeks to provide readers with numerous types of Hawaiian sentences related to the same pictures and vocabulary found in the first book.

For every picture in this book, the reader will find two or more sentences using different structural patterns in Hawaiian. These structural patterns are described in more detail in the Introduction of this book. Readers and students of Hawaiian language can use the *Hawaiian Sentence Book* to expand on the basic vocabulary offered in the *Hawaiian Word Book* and learn how to use that vocabulary to express themselves in more sophisticated Hawaiian phrases.

The sentences should be read out loud and practiced. Audio cassette tapes are available through the Bess Press that contain the words in the *Hawaiian Word Book* and the sentences found in this *Hawaiian Sentence Book*.

E hoʻonanea ʻoukou i ka heluhelu pinepine ʻana i kēia puke ʻōlelo Hawaiʻi liʻiliʻi. He kōkua paha ia iā ʻoukou i ke aʻo ʻana i ka ʻōlelo makuahine o kēia ʻāina. (Enjoy the frequent reading of this little Hawaiian language book. Perhaps it will be a help to you in learning the mother tongue of this land.)

INTRODUCTION

This *Hawaiian Sentence Book* can be used for individual language study or can serve as a text for group learning of the Hawaiian language. In this introduction the general layout of the book and the Hawaiian language structural patterns are described. Suggestions on how to use the book are also included.

The sentences should be read aloud so that correct pronunciation and the rhythmic flow of this beautiful Polynesian language can be perfected. It is highly recommended that readers of the book use the audio cassette tape which accompanies the text and which is available from The Bess Press wherever this book is sold.

The Hawaiian language possesses a relatively simple sound system which can be mastered quickly if a few rules and concepts are kept in mind. It is somewhat traditional to say that the language consists of an alphabet of twelve letters—five vowels and seven consonants.

This is true as far as it goes, but there are two other important aspects to the language which do not exist in English and which must be mastered if the language is to be pronounced correctly and pleasingly. These two elements are the glottal stop and the macron.

The glottal stop or *'okina* is found in many of the Polynesian languages as well as in Arabic and some other languages. It is a quick stopping of the flow of air in the glottis which causes two vowels in sequence to be pronounced separately. Since all Hawaiian words end in a vowel and many of them start with a vowel, the musical flow of the language can be heard as sequential vowels are run together in breath groups or phrases. Glottal stops at the beginning or within words break up this flow and are very important to the correct understanding of words which seem to be spelled similarly.

In Hawaiian, the glottal stop or *'okina* replaces the sound /k/ found in cognate words in a number of southern Polynesian languages such as Maori and Rarotongan.

Some examples that show the importance of the *'okina* in differentiating the meanings of Hawaiian words can be seen in the following pairs:

ko'u	my	kou	your
ma'i	sick	mai	direction toward the speaker
'ahi	tuna	ahi	fire
'awa	kava plant	awa	harbor
'ala	fragrance	ala	road, path
ho'i	to return	hoi	yam
mali'u	well salted	maliu	to turn toward

The macron or *kahakō* indicates that the vowel over which it is placed takes two beats of length instead of just one. Most of the other Polynesian languages as well as Japanese have this feature of pronunciation whereby a short pronunciation of the vowel changes the meaning completely.

Some examples of this important element of the Hawaiian language can be seen in the following words:

nana	to plait	nānā	for him/her
nanā	to strut	nānā	to look at, observe
kau	to place	kāu	your
wahine	woman	wāhine	women
makua	parent	mākua	parents
kumu	teacher	kūmū	goatfish
lulu	calm	lūlū	to scatter

One of the best examples of the changes in pronunciation and, consequently, meaning that are indicated by the use of the two diacritical marks is the following:

pau	completed, finished
pa'u	soot; drudgery
pa'ū	moist, damp, mouldy
pā'ū	traditional woman's wraparound garment; long skirt worn by female horseback riders

The sounds of the five vowels are similar to the vowel sounds in Japanese, Latin and Spanish. They should be pronounced as pure sounds with no off-glides. English speakers especially have a tendency to pronounce the sound /e/ as /ei/ and the sound /o/ as /ou/. Be aware of this tendency and strive to retain the correct initial pronunciation of each of these sounds.

English speakers will also have difficulty pronouncing three vowel clusters correctly unless care is taken. The three sets of minimal pairs are as follows:

Tense sound	Relaxed sound
ai	ae
au	ao
oi	oe

There are many words that can be used to contrast these different vowel cluster sounds. Listen to and practice the difference in sounds in the following word pairs:

mai	(directional)	mae	(faded, wilted)
'ai	(to eat)	'ae	(yes, to agree)

kai	(ocean, sea)	kae	(excrement)
au	(I)	ao	(light, dawn)
hau	(snow)	hao	(iron)
kau	(to place)	kao	(goat)
'oi	(sharp; to excel)	'oe	(you, singular)
moi	(threadfish)	moe	(to lie down)
poi	(mashed taro)	poe	(round)

The Hawaiian consonants are very similar to those in English. One should be aware, however, that the *w* can be sounded as a /w/ or a /v/ depending on its environment in a word. When the *w* is the initial sound or follows the sound /a/, either of the two pronunciations may be used according to common, local usage. After the sounds /e/ and /i/, the *w* is generally pronounced as a /v/ and after the sounds /o/ and /u/, it is generally pronounced as a /w/. This latter rule is especially important in pronouncing such words as *uwē, auwē* and *kauwā* where the *w* should NEVER be pronounced as a /v/ since it is merely a glide sound. In modern spelling, this *w* glide is usually left out of the word.

SENTENCE PATTERNS

The sentence patterns used in this *Hawaiian Sentence Book* may be generally categorized as follows:

1. Equational sentences
2. Descriptive sentences using stative verbs/predicate adjectives
3. *Aia* locational sentences
4. Active verb sentences, both transitive and intransitive
5. Passive verb sentences

Examples of each of these types of sentences and a short discussion of their usage follow below. Readers should note that word order in the Hawaiian sentences is usually different than that in the English translations with the exception of some locational sentences. This difference adds to the interest in learning a new language. The word order in the various kinds of Hawaiian sentences can be quickly learned if the patterns illustrated below are studied and memorized early in one's study of the Hawaiian language.

Because the structure of the Hawaiian language is relatively simple, the importance of the many particles or function words such as 'o, i, e, ma, 'ia, iā, etc. can not be overemphasized. The many uses of these small words should be noticed and studied so that the student may learn to create new sentences correctly based on the material presented in this book.

The *Hawaiian Sentence Book* is not meant to be a grammar of the Hawaiian language nor is it designed to take the place of a good Hawaiian language textbook. This is meant to be a supplementary resource work for students and teachers to use as the Hawaiian language is studied.

1. Equational Sentences

Equational sentences generally contain two parts which are equal. This type of pattern includes identificative, demonstrative and possessive sentences. The pattern can be used when you want to identify who or what someone is; to point out what this or that is; and, to indicate who has something. Each of these types of sentence starts with the indefinite article *he* (a, an) or the subject marker *'o* (no meaning).

a. Identificative sentences indicate who or what someone is. They usually end in a personal pronoun, a person's name preceded by *'o*, or a common noun preceded by a noun marker:

    He wahine u'i 'o ia. (She is a beautiful woman.)
    He wahine u'i 'o Noelani. (Noelani is a beautiful woman.)
    He wahine u'i ko'u makuahine. (My mother is a beautiful woman.)
    'O ko'u makua kāne 'o ia. (He is my father.)
    'O nā haumāna maika'i lākou. (They are the good students.)

    'O ku'u ipo 'o Kauanoe. (My sweetheart is Kauanoe.)
    'O Kauanoe ku'u ipo. (Kauanoe is my sweetheart.)

Because these sentences are equational, the right and left sides of the sentences can be interchanged. It must be remembered, however, that the sentence must start with *he* or *'o*.

    'O ia he wahine u'i. (She is a beautiful woman.)
    'O ko'u makuahine he wahine u'i. (My mother is a beautiful woman.)
    'O lākou nā haumāna maika'i. (They are the good students.)

The rule of thumb to remember with equational sentences, as well as with most Hawaiian utterances, is that the most important thing, person or idea is mentioned first. The language is flexible enough to allow you to make the various sentences as shown above according to what you want to stress in the sentence.

b. Demonstrative sentences show what this or that is. In English we just have two singular demonstratives: this and that. In Hawaiian we have three: this (kēia), that by you *(kēnā)*, and that away from both of us *(kēlā)*.

    He kahuna kēia. (This is a priest.)
    He mau mākua kēia. (These are parents.)
    'O ka 'uala kēia. (This is the sweet potato.)
    He kumulā'au kēlā. (That [over there] is a tree.)
    He mu'umu'u nani kēnā. (That [by you] is a pretty *mu'umu'u*.)
    'O ka mu'umu'u nani kēnā. (That [by you] is the pretty *mu'umu'u*.)
    'O nā mu'umu'u nani kēnā. (Those [by you] are the pretty *mu'umu'u*.)

    Note that there is no special form in Hawaiian for the plural demonstratives: these and those. They become plural when the noun is pluralized using *he mau* or *'o nā*.

c. Possessive sentences indicate who has something. The general pattern is as follows:

> He + thing possessed (+ adjective) + ko/kā + possessor
> He mana ikaika kona. (He has strong power.)
> He pāʻū hou ko kāna kaikamahine. (Her daughter has a new sarong.)
> He mau ʻano puka ko kēia mau kiʻi. (These pictures have some kinds of perforations.)
> He lei kona ma luna o ka pāpale. (She has a garland on the hat.)
> He keiki nani kā kēlā wahine. (That lady has a beautiful child.)
> He kālā kāu ? (Do you have money?)

The possessive markers *ko/kā* indicate the idea of has or have in this pattern even though there is no verb to have in the Hawaiian language. The form *ko* is used with things that fall in the categories of things the Hawaiians and other Polynesians believed humans had a birthright to: body, emotions, shelter, transportation, name, god, chief, ancestors and family, and some others. The form *kā* is used with things that fall into the categories of things acquired after birth: food, money, family members starting with sweetheart and going through husband/wife and children down to grandchildren and descendants.

The possessive system must be studied in greater detail than the brief aspect of it presented above. It is one of only two areas that usually give beginning students some problems if they don't study carefully. The other area is the plethora of particles or function words as mentioned in an earlier section.

In the possessive pattern, the *ko* or *kā* usually is written as a separate particle except when dealing with the first, second and third persons singular (I have, you have, he/she/it has). In these three cases, the *ko/kā* contracts with the possessor to form the following predicate possessives:

koʻu/kaʻu	I have
kou/kāu	You have
kona/kāna	He/she/it has

2. Descriptive Sentences

Descriptive sentences are used to tell what someone or something is like. The descriptive word is called an adjective by some people and a stative verb by others. It is the same thing, i.e., it is a word used to describe the state of someone or something. In English, the sentence pattern is usually:

> Subject + Verb "to be" + Predicate Adjective

In Hawaiian, the rule of thumb about putting the most important thing first is followed in the sentence pattern used for descriptive sentences:

> Predicate Adjective/Stative Verb + Noun/Subject Marker + Subject
> Ua loea kēia keiki kāne (i ka heʻenalu ʻana) This boy is skilled (at surfing).

Huhū ka makuahine. The mother is angry.
Ua mākaukau paha ka meaʻai. Maybe the food is ready.
Ua momona kona kino. Her body is fat.

If the subject is a pronoun, there generally will not be any subject or noun marker before it:

Ua māluhiluhi loa ʻo ia. He is very tired.
Pōloli ʻo ia. He is hungry.

Speakers of Hawaiian Creole English or "pidgin" will note that this is the same pattern we use to say things like: "Good, dis crab!" or "Nice, dat girl!" The "pidgin" pattern seems to have been created by Hawaiians' sticking English words into a thought pattern that they already were using in speaking Hawaiian. So now you just have to reverse the process and think in "pidgin" while inserting the Hawaiian vocabulary!

3. *Aia* Locational Sentences

Sentences used to indicate where something is located are among the simplest to make for the beginning student. Usually the sentence is made by starting off with *aia* (there is/are) or *eia* (here is/are) and then giving the Hawaiian words in the same order as in English.

Aia ke kahakai ma kaʻe o ke kai. There is the beach on the edge of the sea.
Aia ʻekolu kānaka i luna o ka waʻa kaukahi. There are three people aboard the single-hulled canoe.
Eia kekahi mau pāʻani a nā keiki... Here are some of the children's games...
Aia kekahi ʻīlio e pāʻani nei ma waho o ka hīnaʻi. There is a dog playing outside of the basket.

See the section of this book which deals with relative locations for the locative or location words frequently used in locational sentences. It is important to note that the *aia/eia* do not always have to be translated into English but that one of these words MUST be in the Hawaiian sentence, even if the words "there is/are" or "here is/are" are not in the English sentence to be translated.

4. Active Verb Sentences

Verbal sentences that include verbs of action are very important and common in Hawaiian. The pattern is used whenever you wish to tell about someone doing something in the past, present or future. Hawaiian sentences of this type differ from those in English and other European languages because the verb, the most important idea usually, is said before the subject and because Hawaiian does not really have past or future tenses.

The pattern for this type of sentence is quite simple and is the same whether used by itself without reference to time or used with any of the four verbal markers. It is as follows:

Verb + Subject (+ *i/iā* + Object)
Kū ke kaikamahine i luna. The girl is standing up.
'Ike ke keiki kāne i ka lo'i kalo. The boy sees the *taro* patch.

Hawaiian has something called aspect which indicates whether the action is completed or non-completed. There is a way to show the present tense. The verbal marker, *ke ... nei*, is used around the verb. To show the other tenses, however, Hawaiian uses adverbial expressions of time.

The verbal marker, *e ... ana*, is placed around the verb when the noncompleted aspect is to be indicated. The completed aspect is shown by the use of the verbal marker, *ua*, before the verb at the beginning of a phrase. When the verb is inside of the sentence for various reasons, the *ua* changes to *i* to show completed action.

The examples in this section show transitive verbs or those which take an object. Examples using all four verbal markers are shown:

E hoe aku ana lākou i ka wa'a i ka moana. They are going to paddle the canoe to the deep sea.
Ke nānā aku nei 'o ia i nā manu. He is looking at the birds.
Ua 'ai ka po'e Hawai'i i ka 'ulu. Hawaiians ate breadfruit.
Na ka wahine i kuku i ka wauke. It was the woman who beat the indian mulberry.

Other verbs are called intransitive which means that they do not take an object. These examples show the verbal markers used in intransitive verbal sentences:

Ke moe nei kona kaikunāne ma lalo o ke kumu niu. Her brother is reclining/lying down under the coconut tree.
Ua hana nā kāne i ka lo'i kalo. The men worked in the *taro* patch.
E pā'ani pū ana lāua i kēia lā. They two will play together today.

Another verbal marker used with action verbs is the imperative or command marker, *e*. This marker is placed before the verb and is expressed orally with a tone of voice indicating that someone should do whatever action is stated.

E nānā i ka holu nape a ka lau o ka niu. Look at the swaying of the coconut fronds.
E ho'omau i ka helu 'ana a hiki i 'umi. Continue counting to ten.

5. Passive Verb Sentences

Passive verb sentences use the action verb in the passive voice. Passive voice has nothing to do with past tense. It is a device which exists in English, Hawaiian and many other languages to focus attention on the recipient of an action (the object) by moving it to the beginning of the sentence.

Active voice: Keola prepared the *imu.* Keola is preparing the *imu.*

Passive voice: The *imu* was prepared by Keola. The *imu* is being prepared by Keola.

These examples show passive voice sentences in the past and present tenses. The passive voice can also be used in the future tense in English. In Hawaiian, the passive voice can likewise be used with the verbal markers, *ke ... nei, e ... ana,* and *ua.* Two examples from this book both use the completed action marker, *ua.*

Ua hana 'ia ke alaia i ka 'ulu, ke koa a me ka wiliwili i ka wā kahiko. The short board was made of breadfruit, *Acacia koa* and *Erythrina sandwicensis* in the old days.

Ua kūkulu 'ia ka hale ma luna o ka paepae pōhaku. The house was built on a stone foundation.

The verb marker that indicates the passive voice is *'ia,* which is written right after the verb but separated from it. When using *e ... ana* or *ke ... nei,* the passive marker, *'ia,* is put with the verb between the two parts of the verbal markers.

There are other structural elements of the Hawaiian language which must be learned at some point by the student of the language. It is not important that they be explained in this introduction. Serious language students should seek further explanations in the various textbooks and grammars of the Hawaiian language which are available in bookstores and libraries.

The five types of sentence patterns described in these pages are the most common and most important that the beginning students will need to know in order to communicate complete thoughts in the Hawaiian language. The examples should be read aloud so that the patterns may become familiar to the ear. Students may wish to try to identify which sentences fit which patterns as they go through sections of this book. Numerous examples of all of the patterns except the passive voice sentences may be found throughout the book.

E holomua i ke a'o 'ana i ka 'ōlelo Hawai'i me ke akahele a me ka pa'ahana a lilo i kanaka poeko. Move forward in studying the Hawaiian language cautiously and industriously so that you may become a person who is fluent and clever in speaking.

Ko Ka Poʻe Kānaka
About People

akua	kauā	mākua
aliʻi	keiki (kama)	makua kāne
aloha	keiki kāne	makua kāne hanauna
hale	kiʻi	makuahine
hoahānau	kupuna	makuahine hanauna
inoa	kūpuna	moena
kahuna	kupuna kāne	ʻohana
kaikamahine	kupuna wahine	uluna
kamaiki	lei	pūhā
kanaka	mahalo	puka
kānaka	makaʻāinana	pukaaniani
kāne	makua	wahine
		wāhine

AKUA

He kiʻi lāʻau kēia.
He kiʻi akua kēia.
ʻO kēia kiʻi he hōʻailona o ke akua, ʻo Kū.
I ka wā kahiko, ʻo ke kiʻi he hōʻailona o ka mana o nā akua.

ALI‘I

He po‘e ali‘i kēia.
‘A‘ahu ke ali‘i kāne i ka ‘ahu‘ula.
Aia ka mahiole ma luna o kona po‘o.
Ua hume ‘o ia i ka malo.
Aia ka pe‘ahi i ka lima ‘ākau o ke ali‘i wahine.
Ua lei ‘o ia i ka lei niho palaoa.
Ua kau ka lei hulu ma luna o ke po‘o.

KAHUNA

He kahuna kēia.
He mana ikaika kona.
He nui nā ʻano kāhuna i ka wā kahiko.

MAKA'ĀINANA

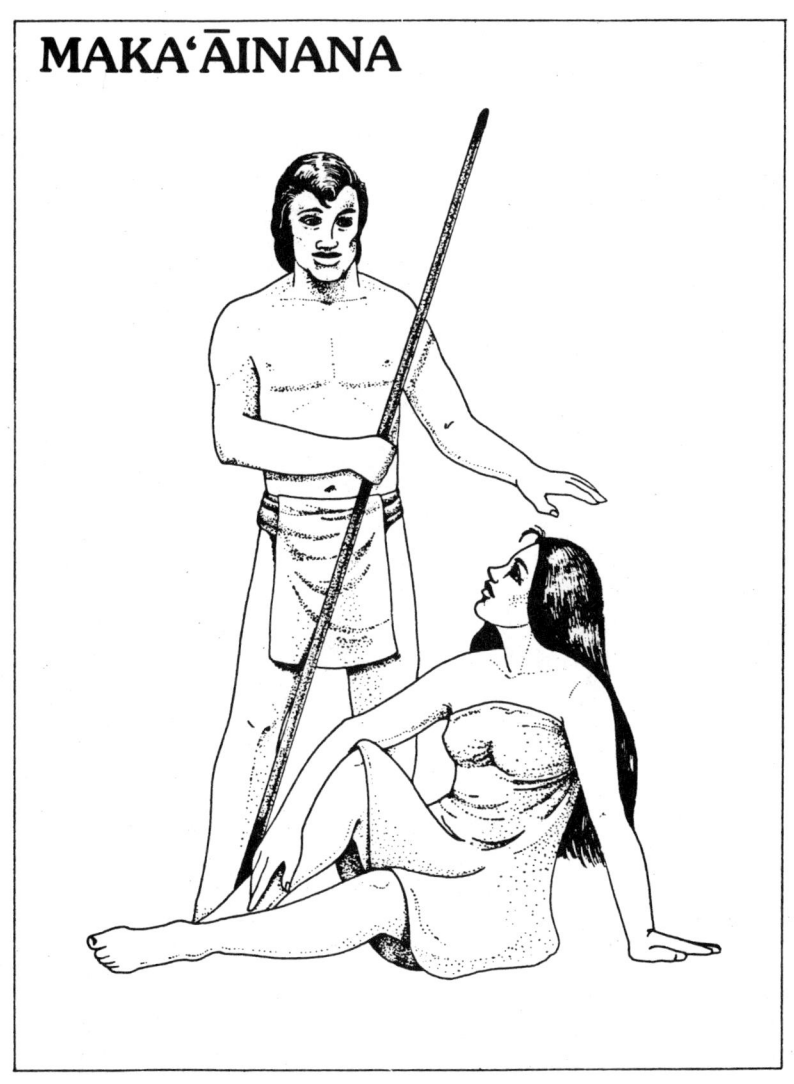

He poʻe makaʻāinana kēia.
He kanaka mahiʻai paha ke kāne.
Aia ka ʻōʻō i kona lima ʻākau.
Ua hume ʻo ia i ka malo.
Noho ka wahine i lalo.
Ua komo ʻo ia i ka pāʻū.
Ua lōʻihi kona lauoho.
He wahine uʻi ʻo ia.

KAUĀ (KAUWĀ)

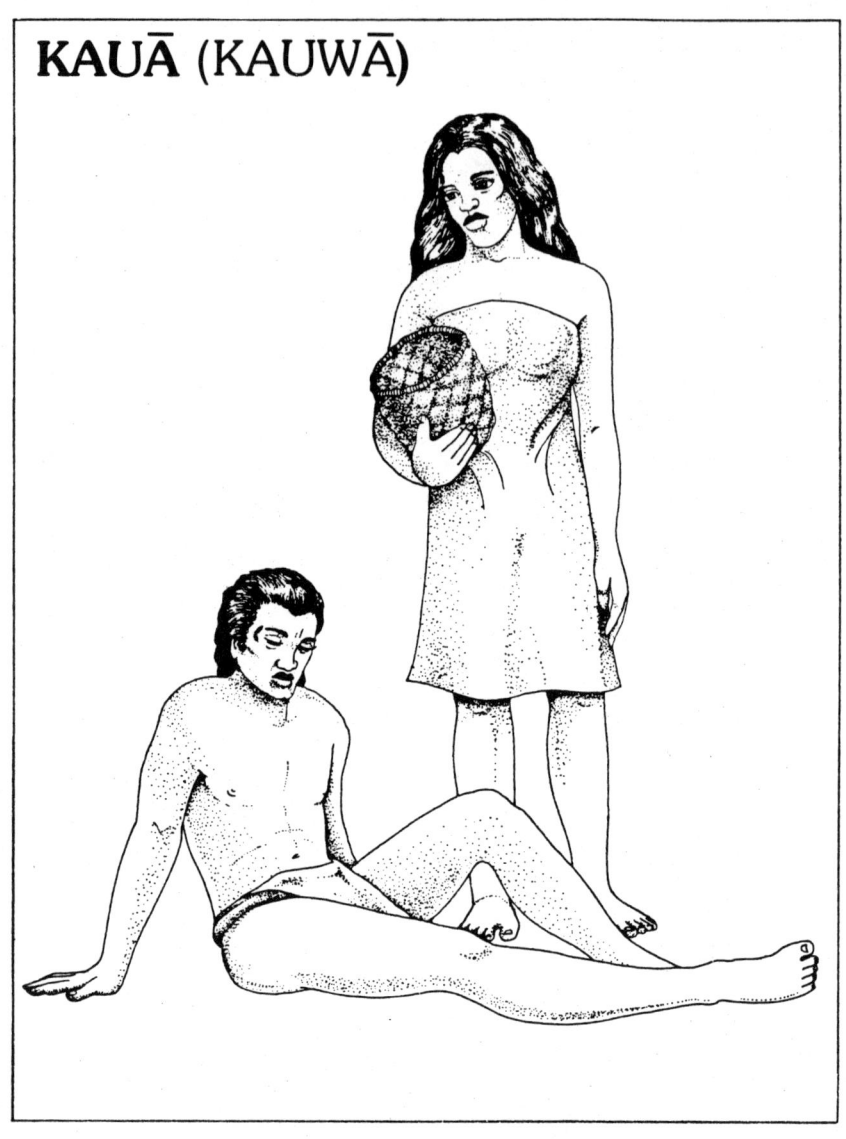

He poʻe kauā kēia.
Ua pio paha lāua i ke kaua.
Ua kākau ʻia lāua i ka hikoni ma ka helehelena.
He hōʻailona kēlā o ko lāua kūlana.

'O nā inoa ke kumuhana o kēia kiʻi.
'O Kekoa ka inoa o ke keiki kāne.
'O Kuʻulei lāua ʻo Mokihana nā inoa o nā kaikamāhine.
'O wai kou inoa?
'O wai ka inoa o ka ʻīlio?

KANAKA

He kanaka kēia.
Hoʻokahi nō ʻo ia.
Ke kū nei ʻo ia me ka ihe ma ka lima ʻākau.
Ua hume ʻo ia i ka malo.

KĀNAKA

He mau kānaka kēia.
Aia i loko o ke ki'i, 'ehā kāne, 'elua wāhine,
'ehā keiki kāne a me ho'okahi kaikamahine.
He po'e Hawai'i kēia mau kānaka.

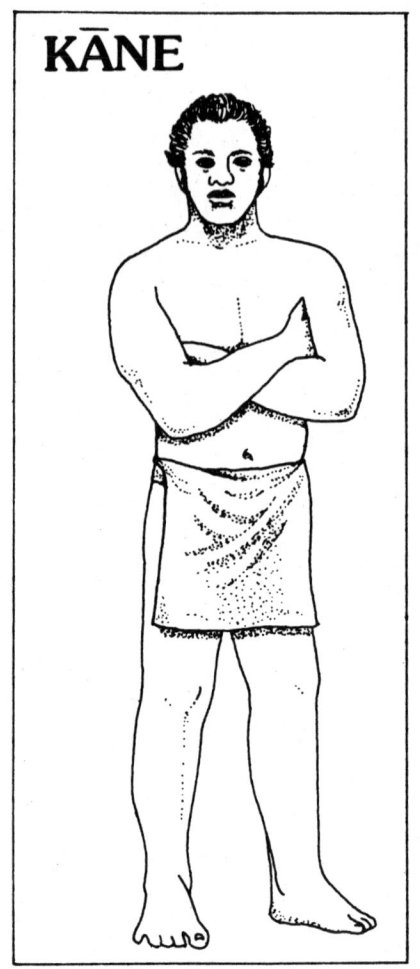

He kāne kēia.
Ua hume ʻo ia i ka malo.
Ua kāpeʻapeʻa nā lima.
He konohiki paha ʻo ia.

KĀNE

He mau kāne kēia.
E kūkākūkā ana lākou i ka malu o ka niu.

He wahine kēia.
Ua komo ʻo ia i ka pāʻū me ke kīhei ma ka poʻohiwi hema.
Ua uʻi kēia wahine i kona lauoho lōʻihi.

He mau wāhine kēia.
Aia ʻelua o lākou e kū ana i luna.
Aia ʻekolu o lākou e noho ana i lalo.
Ua ākoakoa lākou ma mua o ka hale.

'O ka lei ke kumuhana o kēia ki'i.
Ke lei nei ka wahine i ke kāne i ka lei maile.
Aia ka lei po'o ma ke po'o o ka wahine.
He lei pua kēlā.
Aloha aku ka wahine i ke kāne.
Mahalo aku ke kāne i ka wahine.

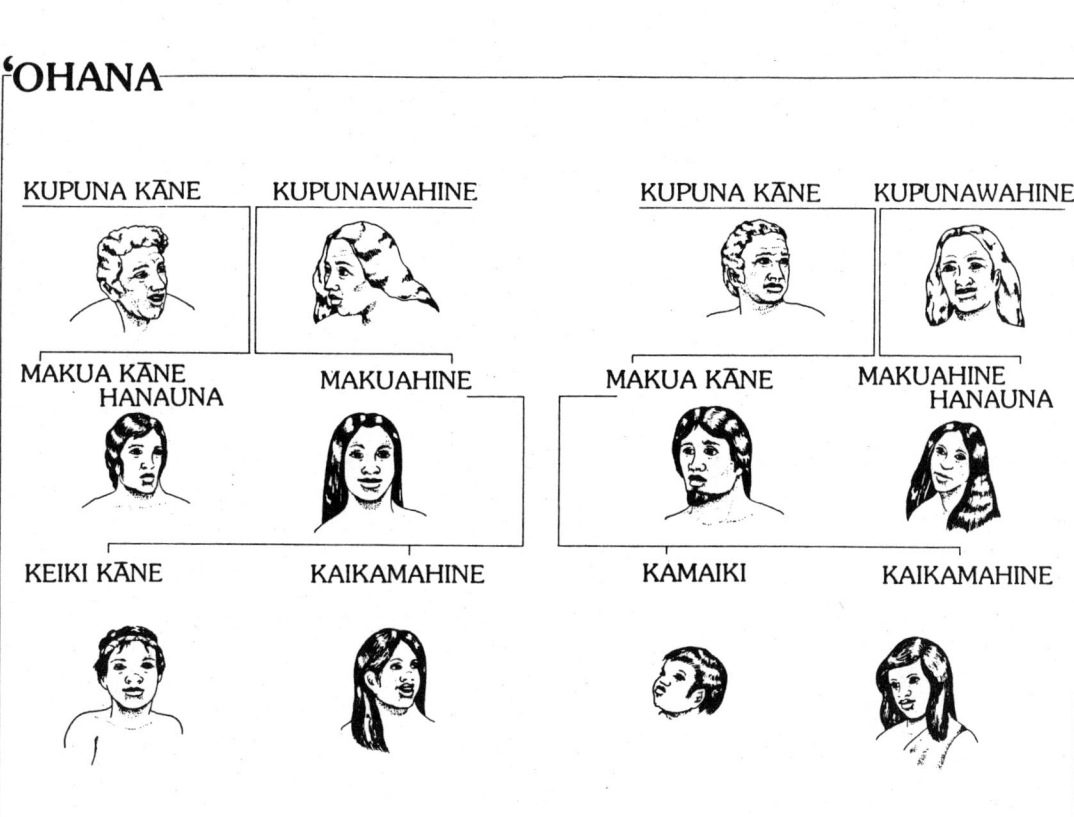

He ʻohana Hawaiʻi kēia.
He moʻokūʻauhau kēia.
Aia nā kūpuna ʻehā, ka makuahine me kona kaikunāne, ka makua kāne me kona kaikuahine, a me nā keiki ʻehā.
Aia ʻelua kaikamāhine, hoʻokahi keiki kāne, a me hoʻokahi kamaiki kāne i loko o kēia ʻohana.

He kupuna kēia.
He kupuna wahine ʻo ia.
Aia ʻo ia e kū ana me kāna moʻopuna kāne.
Ua komo ʻo ia i ka pāʻū me ke kīhei ma ka poʻohiwi hema.
Ua hauʻoli ke keiki kāne.

He mau kūpuna kēia.
Aia ke kupuna wahine a me ke kupuna kāne
e noho ana i ka malu o nā niu.
He ʻelemakule ke kupuna kāne.
He luahine ke kupuna wahine.
Ke hoʻomaha paha nei lāua.

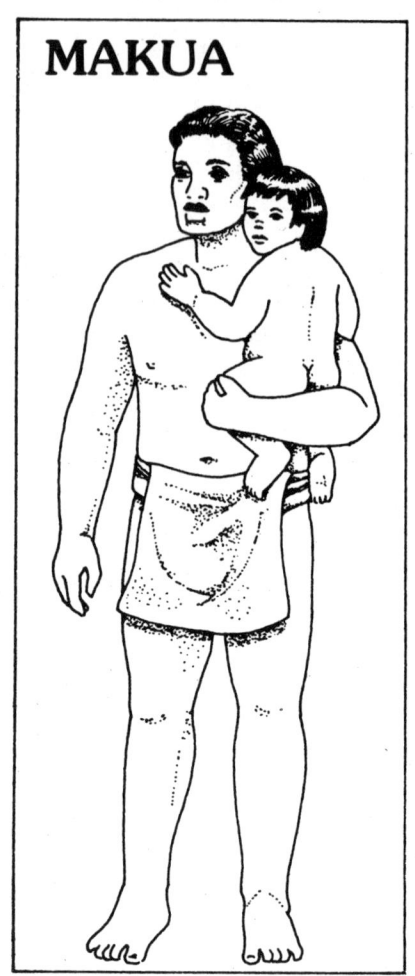

He makua kēia.
He makua kāne ʻo ia.
Ke hāpai nei ʻo ia i kāna kamaiki i ka lima hema.
Ua aloha ka makua kāne i kāna keiki.

MĀKUA

He mau mākua kēia.
Aia ʻekolu mākua kāne a me ʻelua mākuahine i loko o ke kiʻi.
Aia ka makua kāne e kū ana me kona kaikaina a me kona hoahānau.
Aia ka makuahine e kuku ana i ke kapa.
Aia ʻo ia e noho ana i lalo me kona kaikuaʻana.

KEIKI (KAMA)

He poʻe keiki kēia.
Aia hoʻokahi kaikamahine, hoʻokahi keiki kāne a me hoʻokahi kamaiki i loko o ke kiʻi.
Aia nā kamaliʻi e kū ana i luna
Aia ke kamaiki e noho ana i lalo ma ka mauʻu.
Ua kau ka pua kokiʻo ma ka pepeiao ʻākau o ke kaikamahine.

HALE

'O ka hale pili kēia. I ka wā ma mua, ua noho ka poʻe Hawaiʻi i kauhale. Aia kekahi hale kūpono no kekahi hana. Eia kekahi mau ʻano hale: ka hale mua, ka hale ʻaina, ka hale noa, ka hale kahūmu, ka hale peʻa, ka hale kuku, a pēlā wale aku. Ua kūkulu ʻia ka hale ma luna o ka paepae pōhaku. Loaʻa mau nā paepae hale o ka wā kahiko i nā wahi like ʻole a hiki i kēia mau lā.

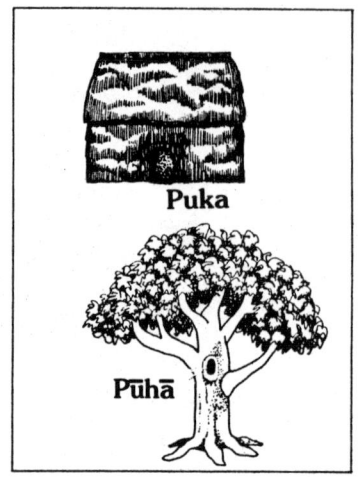 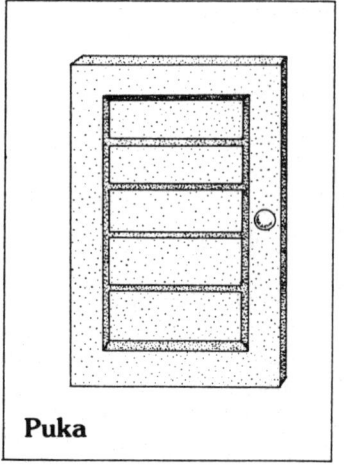

He mau ʻano puka ko kēia mau kiʻi. I ka wā kahiko, ua komo ka poʻe i loko o ka hale ma ka puka. He puka maoli ia i loko o ka paia o ka hale. I kēia manawa, aia he papalāʻau a i ʻole he papaaniani no ka pani ʻana i ka puka o ka hale. ʻAʻohe puka o ke kumu lāʻau, ʻo ka huaʻōlelo pololei, he pūhā. Hiki iā ʻoe ke nānā ma o ka pukaaniani o ka hale.

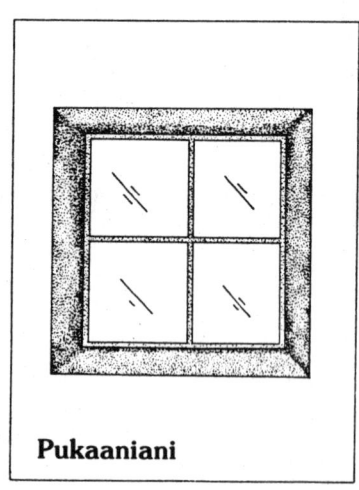

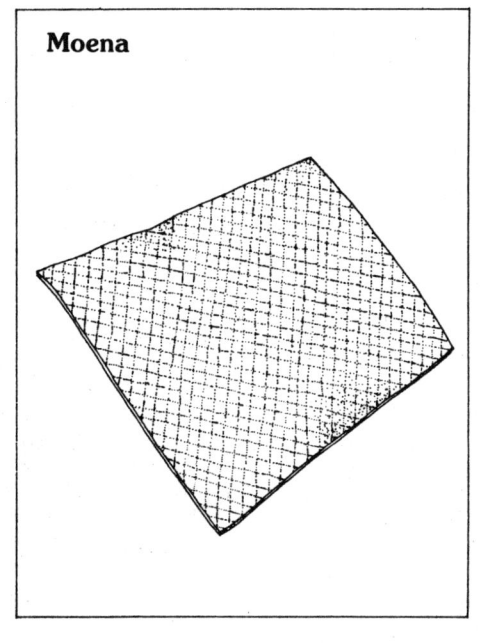

Moena

Uluna

'O ka moena a me ka uluna kēia. Ua noʻeau nā wāhine Hawaiʻi i ka ulana moena ʻana. Ua ulana lākou i nā moena no ka hale, nā uluna lau hala, nā peʻahi, nā ʻeke, a pēlā wale aku. ʻO kēia uluna he uluna ʻano hou. ʻAʻole i hana ʻia i ka lau hala, akā, ua hana ʻia i ka lole me nā hulu. I ka wā ma mua, ua hiamoe ka poʻe Hawaiʻi ma luna o ka moena lau hala, akā, i kēia manawa hiamoe nō kākou i ka wahi moe.

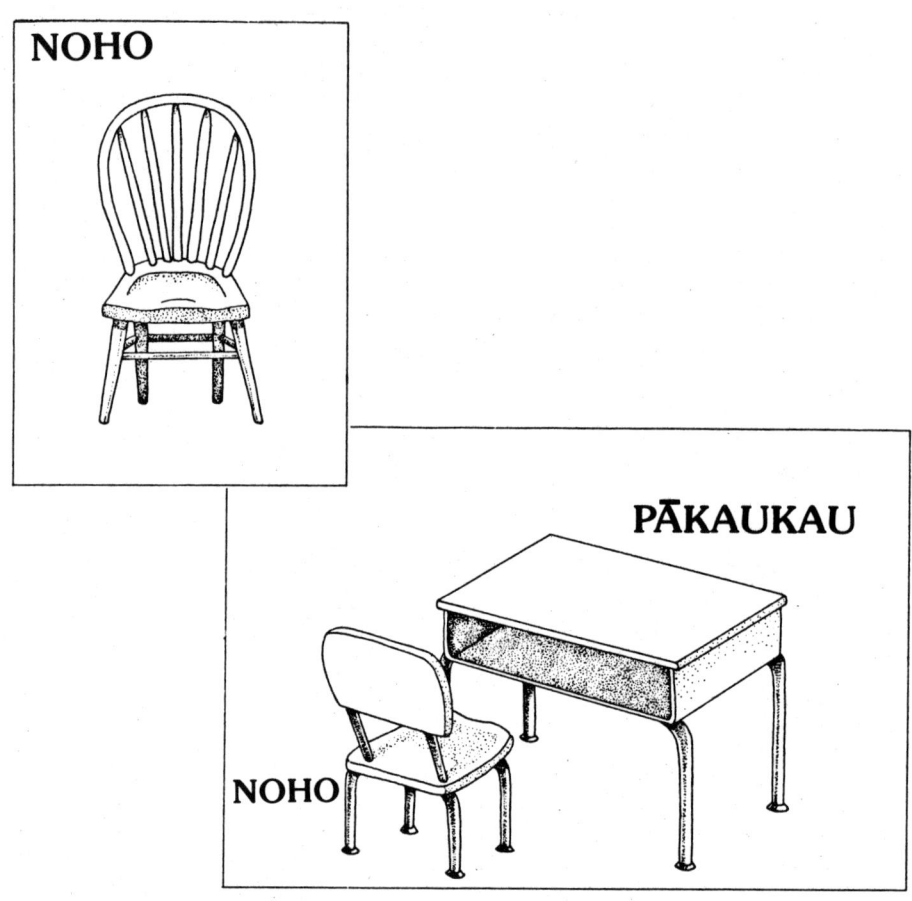

Eia ʻelua ʻano noho. I ka wā ma mua, ua noho ka poʻe Hawaiʻi ma luna o ka moena, ʻaʻole ma ka noho. He mea ia i lawe ʻia mai e ka poʻe Haole. Aia ka noho kula ma hope o ka pākaukau hana. Noho ka haumāna i luna o kēlā ʻano noho i loko o ka lumi kula.

Ke Kino
The Body

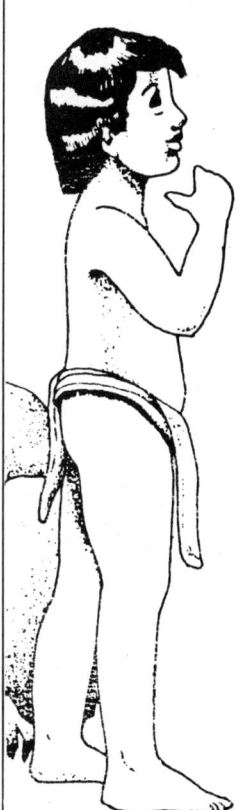

ʻaʻī	kuli	pepeiao
ake	lauoho	piko
ʻauwae	lima	poʻo
ihu	maka	poʻohiwi
iwi	manamana lima	puʻuwai
kīkala	manamana wāwae	ʻūhā
kino	naʻau	umauma
kua	ʻōpū	waha
		wāwae

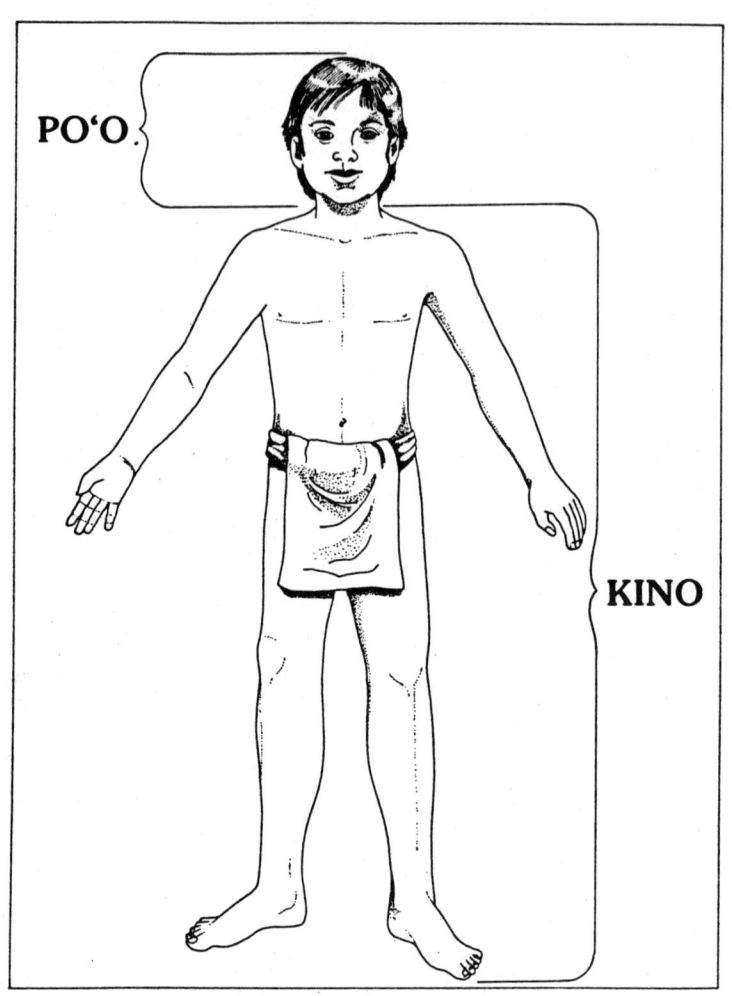

ʻO ke kino o ke kanaka kēia.
Aia ke poʻo ma luna o ke kino.
He keiki kāne kēia.
Hoʻokahi ona poʻo.
ʻElua ona lima.
ʻElua ona wāwae.

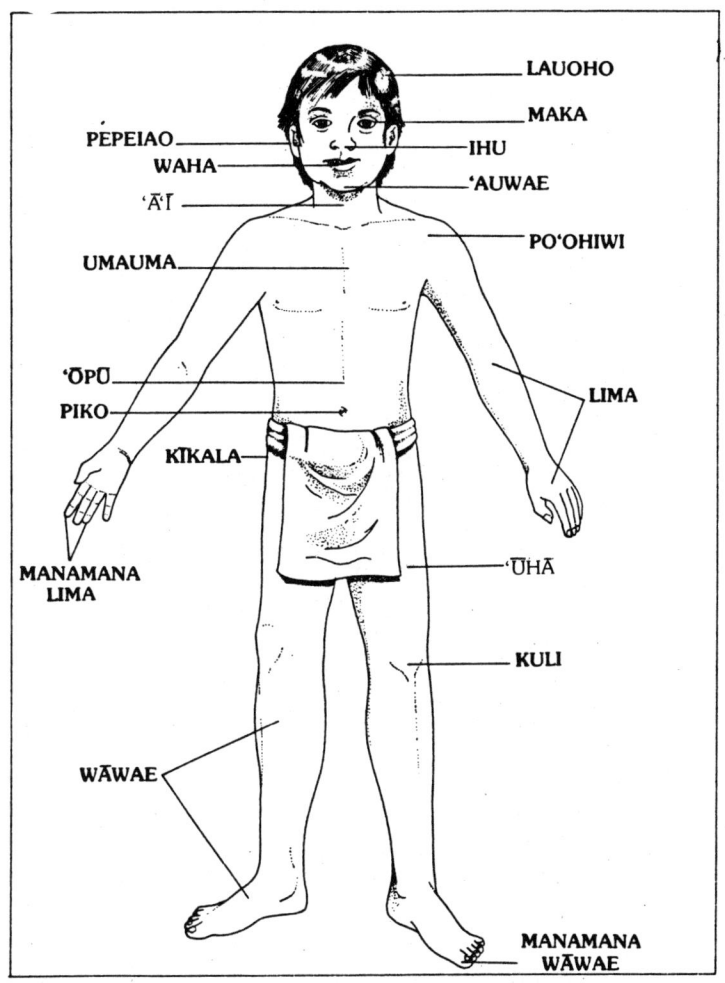

'O ke kino o ke kanaka kēia.
Aia kekahi o nā māhele o ke kino.
'Ehia ona maka? 'Elua ona maka.
'Ehia ona waha? Ho'okahi ona waha.
'Elua ona pepeiao.
Ho'okahi ona ihu.
'Ehia ona manamana lima? He 'umi ona manamana lima.
'Ehia ona manamana wāwae?
He 'umi ona manamana wāwae.

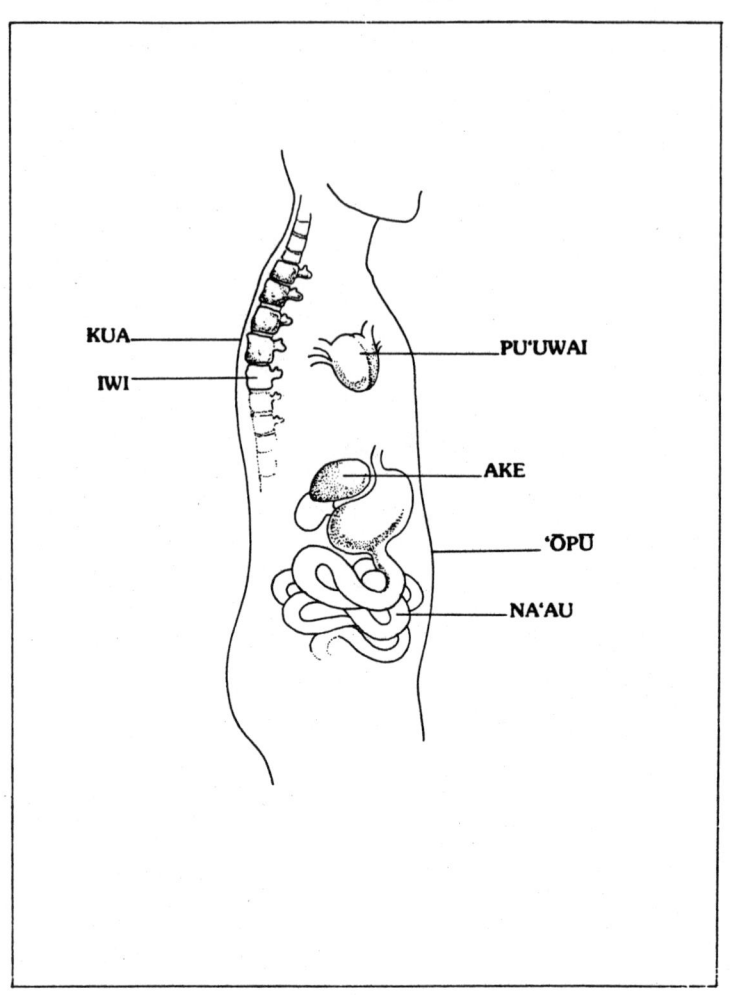

'O kēia kekahi mau māhele o loko o ke kino o ke kanaka.
Aia ke kua i hope o ke kino.
Aia ka pu'uwai ma luna o ka 'ōpū.
Aia ka na'au i lalo o ka 'ōpū.
He nui nā iwi ma loko o ke kino kanaka.

Ka Nohona Hawai'i
Hawaiian Lifestyle

ahi
ahiahi
'ai
ala
ānuenue
'auinalā
awakea
halakahiki
hē'ī
hoe
hōkū
i'a
'īlio
inu
kahakai
kai
kakahiaka
kalo
kō
kuahiwi
kumulā'au
lā
lā'au
lau
lepo
liliko'i
limu
mahina
mai'a
makani
manu
mauna
moa
moana
nalu
niu
one
'ono
pa'i'ai
pali
papa
pele
pō
pōhaku
poi
pua
pua'a
pūpū
ua
'uala
'ulu
wa'a
wailele

'O ka lā kēia.
Pā mai ka lā i ka lā.
Aia ka lā i ka lewa ma luna o ka hale a me nā kumu niu.

ʻO ka pō kēia.
Pā mai ka mahina a me nā hōkū i ka pō.

Ua ala ke kaikamahine i ke kakahiaka.
Ke hoʻomanana nei ʻo ia i nā lima.
Ke hoʻohāmama nei ʻo ia no kona molohai mau.

AWAKEA

Hoʻomaha ke keiki kāne i ke awakea.
Ke piʻi nei ʻo ia i ke kumu niu.
ʻImi ʻo ia i ka wai hōʻolu o ka niu.

Hoʻomākaukau ke kanaka lawaiʻa i kāna ʻupena i ka ʻauinalā.
Makemake paha ʻo ia e hele i ka lawaiʻa.

Napoʻo ka lā i ke ahiahi.
Ke nānā nei kēia poʻe ipo i ka napoʻo ʻana o ka lā.

'O ke ānuenue kēia.
Aia ke ānuenue i ka lewa.
Pi'o mai ke ānuenue, ke ua kilihune i ka lā.
Hau'oli ke kanaka mahi'ai e 'ike i ka ua.
Mana'o 'o ia, "Ua ka ua, ola mai ka nohona o ka 'āina kula."
He mea maika'i loa ka ua no ke kalo.

MAKANI

'O ka makani kēia.
Pā mai ka makani. he lā 'ino ia.
Hao kō'ala ka makani, pau loa.
Hao mai ka makani, kuakea ka moana.

PELE

He mauna kēia e luaʻi ana i ka pele. Aia nā lua pele ma Hawaiʻi nei a i kekahi mau ʻāina ʻēʻaʻe ma kēia honua. Ua manaʻo ka poʻe Hawaiʻi, ʻo Pele ke akua wahine o ka lua pele. Nāna e hoʻonui mau i ka ʻāina ʻo Puna me ka pele e kahe ana i kai.

AHI

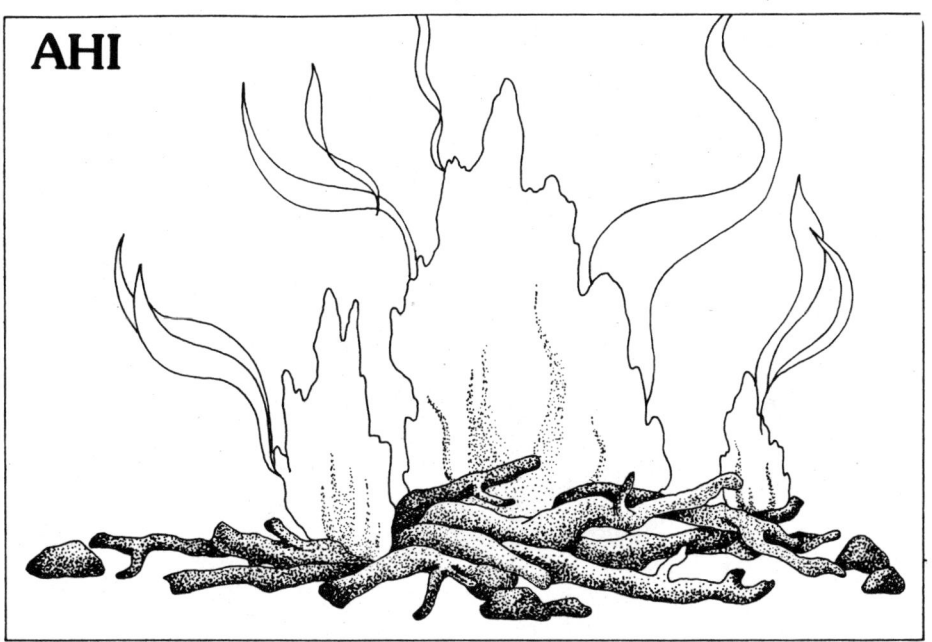

ʻO ke ahi kēia.

Na Maui i haʻawi i ke ahi i ka poʻe kanaka i ka wā ma mua loa. Ua hiki i ka poʻe ke hoʻomoʻa i ka meaʻai.

ʻO ke ahi he mea hoʻomaikaʻi i kekahi manawa a he mea hōʻino i kekahi manawa ʻē aʻe.

E mālama nā keiki i ke ahi o pau ka hale i ke ahi!

Aia nā kuahiwi i nā mokupuni kāhiko, ʻo ia hoʻi, ʻo Kauaʻi lāua ʻo Oʻahu. Aia nā mauna i nā mokupuni ʻano ʻōpio, ʻo ia hoʻi ʻo Maui a me Hawaiʻi. Loaʻa i nā mokupuni a pau nā wailele. He keu a ka nani o nā wailele ma ka ʻaoʻao Koʻolau o Molokaʻi! Kahe ka wai o ke kahawai ma luna o nā pōhaku nui a liʻiliʻi.

Aia nā manu e kīkaha aʻela ana i ka makani mau
o nā pali Koʻolau o nā mokupuni like ʻole.
Ua kiʻekiʻe kēia mau pali.
Aia nā kumulāʻau e ulu ana i luna o nā pali.
Aia hoʻi ka lauaʻe e ulu ana ma lalo o
nā kumulāʻau.

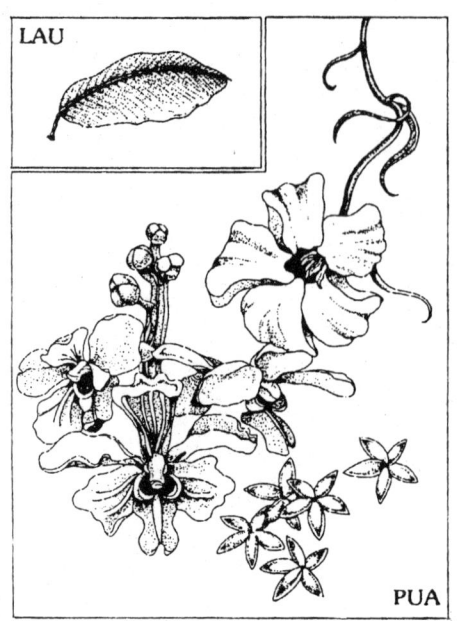

He lau kēia ma ke kiʻi i luna. ʻO ka lau o ka pua melia paha. Ua lawe ʻia mai kēlā lāʻau mai ʻAmelika Waena mai. He nui nā ʻano pua like ʻole ma nā kumulāʻau i Hawaiʻi nei. Ua nani a ʻaʻala ka hapanui o nā pua. Hiki ke hana i nā lei like ʻole me nā pua. Aia ʻekolu ʻano lāʻau ma ke kiʻi. ʻO ke kumulāʻau nui he manakō paha ia. ʻOno loa nā hua o ia kumulāʻau.

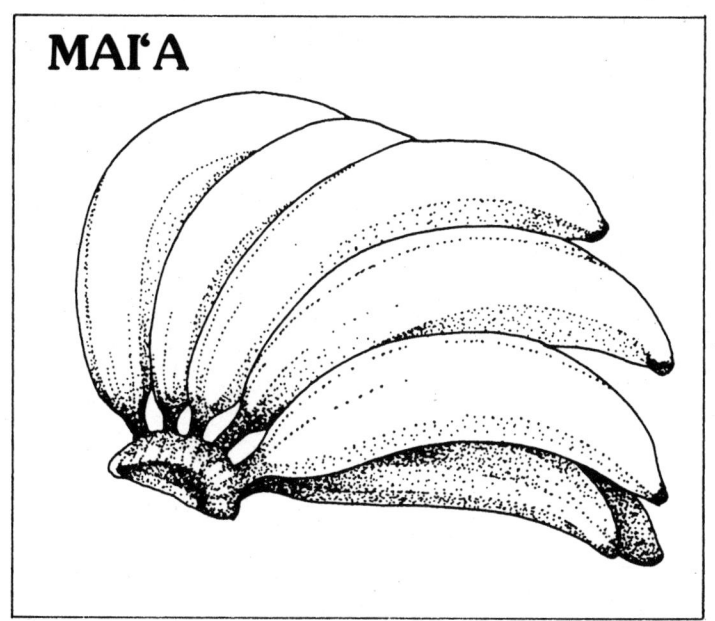

MAIʻA

ʻO ka ʻekā maiʻa kēia.
I ka wā kahiko, he nui nā ʻano maiʻa.
Melemele ka hua pala o ka maiʻa.

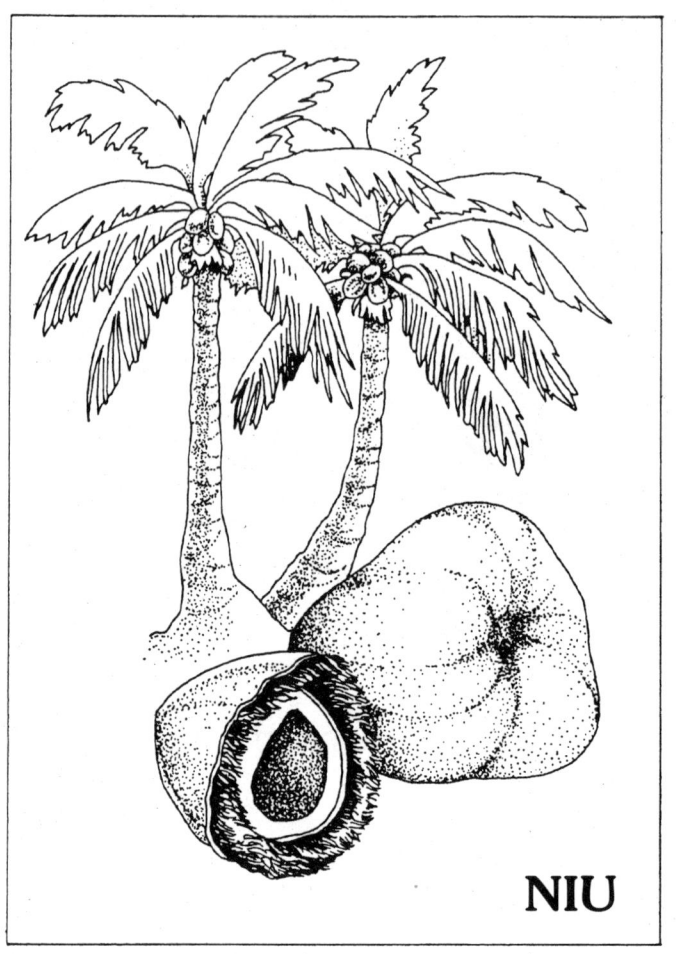

NIU

He mau kumu niu kēia me nā hua.
He nāne ia e pili ana i ka niu:
'Ekolu pā a loa'a ka wai. 'O ia ho'i—ka pulu niu, ka iwi niu a me ka 'i'o niu.

INU

Ke inu nei ke keiki kāne i ka wai niu.
Ua ʻono ka wai niu i ka lā wela.

Ke ʻai nei ke kaikamahine i ka poi.
Ua ʻono maoli ka poi i ka poʻe Hawaiʻi.
ʻO ka poi ka meaʻai koʻikoʻi loa na ka poʻe Hawaiʻi.

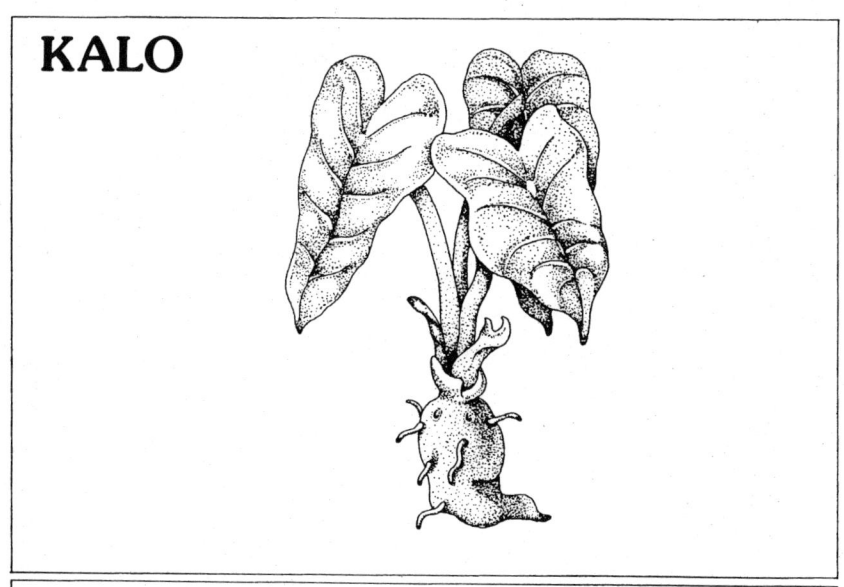

'O ke kalo kēia.
'O ke kalo ka mea kanu nui loa i ka po'e Hawai'i.
Ku'i lākou i ke kalo mo'a no ka pa'i'ai.
Ke ho'owali 'oe i ka wai i ka pa'i'ai, loa'a ka poi.
'Ono loa ka poi me ka i'a.

ALA

Hele wāwae ke kaikamahine ma ke ala. Ke lawe paha mai nei ʻo ia i ka meaʻai i kona mau kaikunāne. Ke hana nei lāua i ka mahina ʻai. Ua lepo ko lāua mau kino. Hoʻopaʻa kekahi o nā keiki kāne i ke kalo ma kona lima hema. Ulu ka ʻuala i ka puʻe lepo.

'ULU

He mau 'ulu kēia.
Ua 'ai ka po'e Hawai'i i ka 'ulu.
Makemake loa ka po'e Kāmoa a me ka po'e Tonga i ka 'ulu.

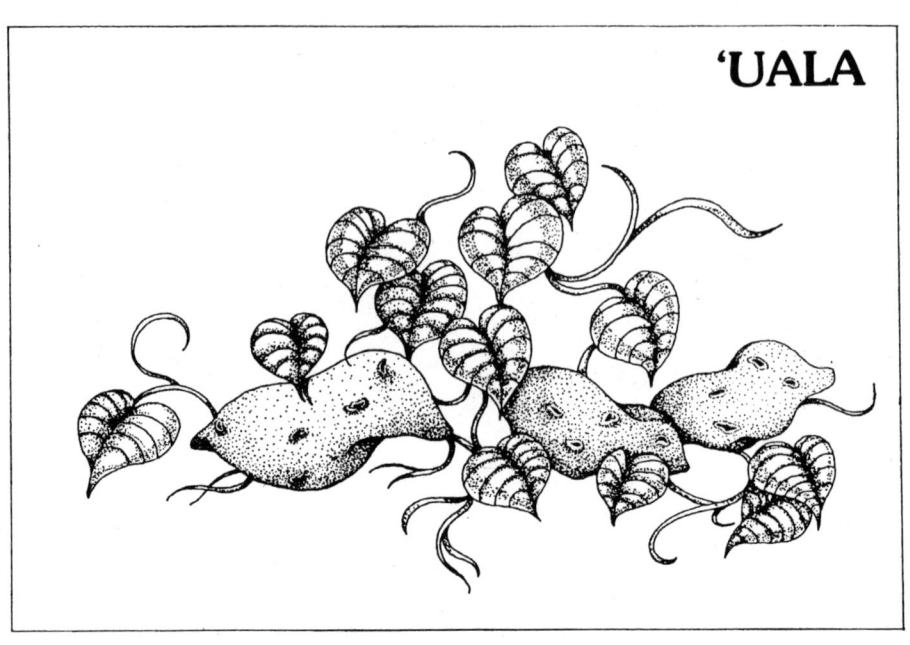

'O ka 'uala kēia.
He mea kanu koʻikoʻi hoʻi no ka poʻe Hawaiʻi.
He kinolau o ke akua ʻo Lono kēia.

'O ke kō kēia.
Ua ulu ke kō i ke au kahiko i Hawai'i.
He nui nō nā 'ano hou e ulu ana i kēia manawa.

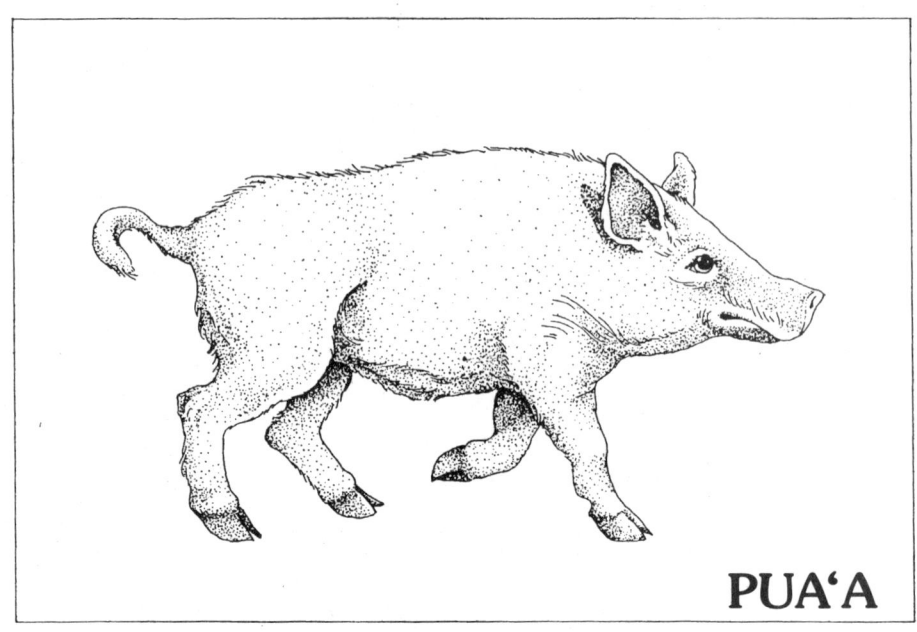

PUAʻA

He puaʻa kēia.
Ua lawe mai ka poʻe Polinekia i ka puaʻa i Hawaiʻi.
Kālua ʻia ka puaʻa i loko o ka imu.
ʻAi kākou i ka puaʻa kālua ma ka pāʻina a i ʻole ma ka lūʻau.

ʻĪLIO

He ʻīlio kēia.
Ua hānai ka poʻe Hawaiʻi i ka ʻīlio no ka ʻai ʻana.
ʻO ke ʻano o ka ʻīlio Hawaiʻi he "poi dog."

He moa kēia.
He moa kāne ia me ka puapua nani.

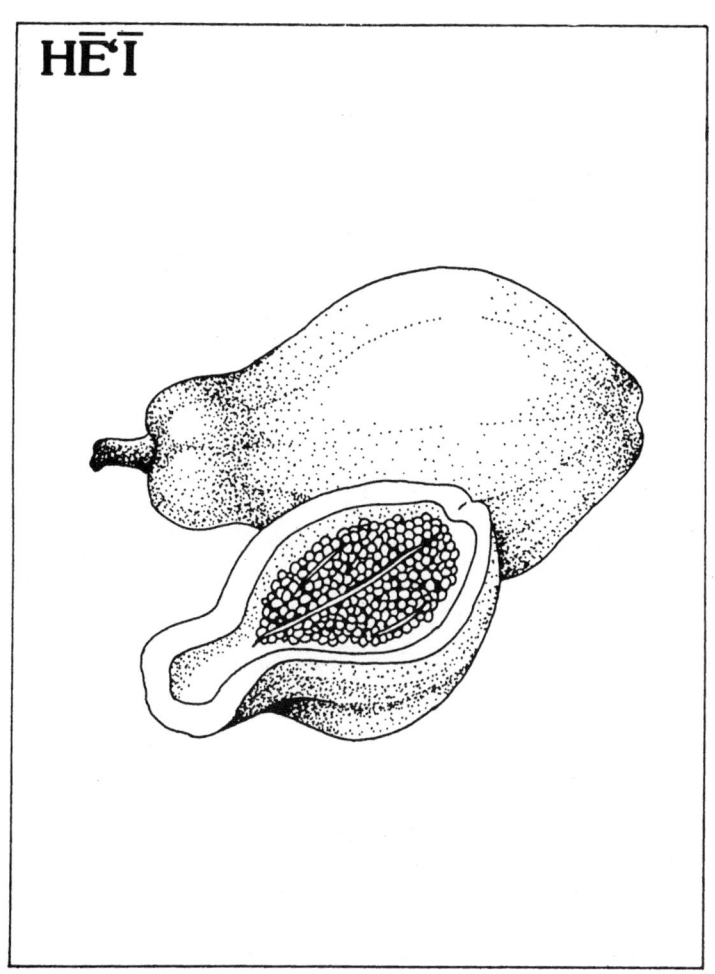

He hēʻī kēia.
ʻO ka mīkana he inoa ʻē aʻe o kēia mea kanu.
Ua ʻono kēia huaʻai no ka ʻaina kakahiaka.

'O ka halakahiki kēia.
He mea kanu nui no kēia au.
Mana'o kekahi po'e, he halakea a he hala'ula ko ka po'e Hawai'i i ka wā ma mua.

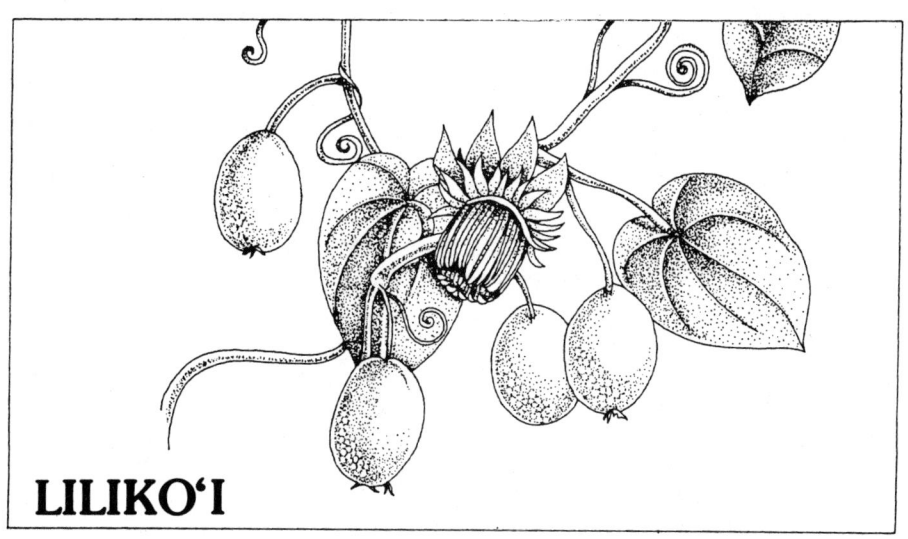

LILIKOʻI

ʻO ka lilikoʻi kēia.
Hiki iā ʻoe ke hana i ka wai huaʻai ʻono maoli me nā hua.

Aia ke kahakai ma kaʻe o ke kai. Hele pinepine ka poʻe Hawaiʻi i kahakai. Makemake mākou e hoʻomoana ma laila. Hiki i nā keiki ke pāʻani i ke one. Hiki i nā mākua ke lawaiʻa i ke kai. Makemake ka hapanui o ka poʻe e ʻauʻau kai.

Aia ʻekolu kānaka i luna o ka waʻa kaukahi.
Aia lākou e hoe ana ma ke kai.
He poʻe lawaiʻa paha lākou.
E hoe aku ana lākou i ka waʻa i ka moana.
E nānā i ke ʻano o ka hoe Hawaiʻi.

He nalu nui kēia.
Ua makemake loa ka poʻe Hawaiʻi e heʻenalu i nā ʻano nalu like ʻole.

PAPA HEʻENALU

He papa heʻenalu kēia.
Ua loea kēia keiki kāne i ka heʻenalu ʻana.
Heʻenalu ʻo ia i nā nalu nunui.
ʻO ke alaia ke ʻano o kona papa heʻenalu.
Ua hana ʻia ke alaia i ka ʻulu, ke koa a me ka wiliwili i ka wā kahiko.

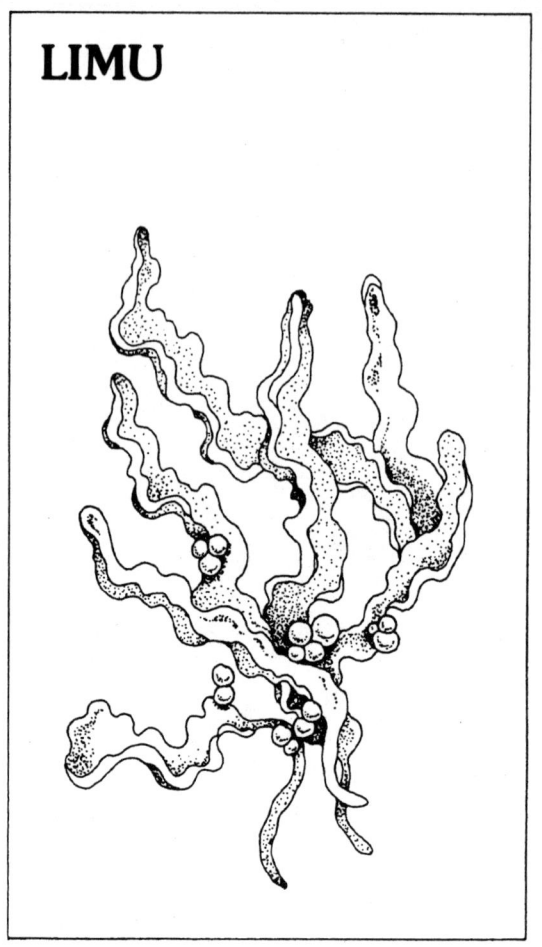

LIMU

'O ka limu kēia.
He mea'ai ko'iko'i kēia mai ke kai mai.
He nui nā 'ano limu.

I'A

He mau iʻa kēia.
ʻO ka iʻa he meaʻai koʻikoʻi na ka poʻe makaʻāinana i ka wā kahiko.
ʻO ka iʻa he meaʻai kūpono no ke olakino maikaʻi.
He nui nā ʻano iʻa i nā kai ʻewalu o Hawaiʻi.

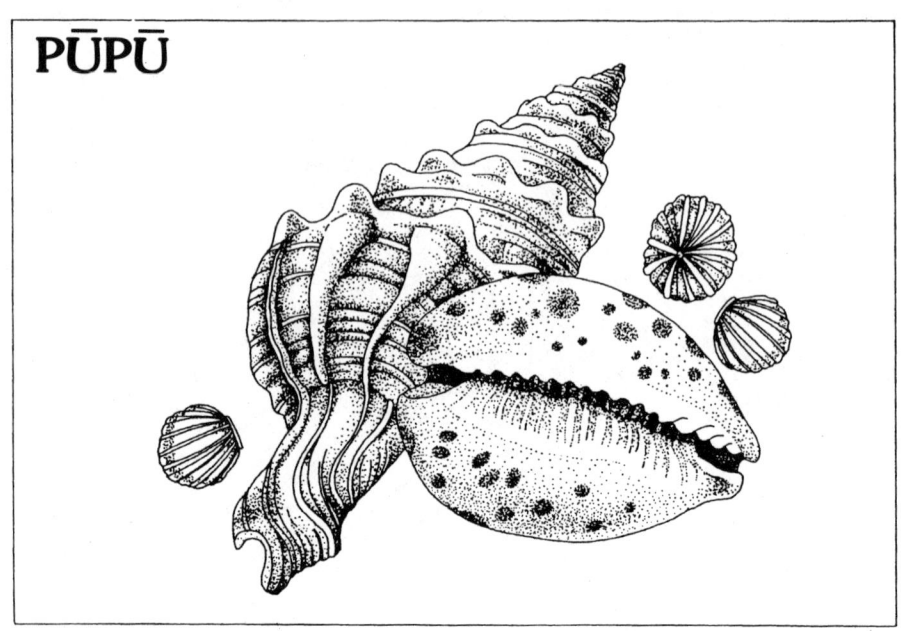

PŪPŪ

He mau pūpū kēia.
He nui nā 'ano pūpū ko nā kai 'ewalu o Hawai'i nei.
'O ka lei pūpū ka lei o Ni'ihau.

HAʻINA
Verbs

Stative verbs/Adjectives	Action verbs
anuanu	ʻauʻau
hauʻoli	hana
ʻino	hele aku
hou	hele mai
kahiko	helu
kaumaha	hiamoe
liʻiliʻi	holo
lōʻihi	hoʻolohe
mālie	ʻike
momona	kū
nani	lele
nui	lohe
pōkole	moe
uʻi	nānā
ʻuʻuku	noho
wela	ʻōlelo
wīwī	

Kū ke kaikamahine i luna. Ke moe nei kona kaikunāne ma lalo o ke kumu niu. Ke nānā aku nei 'o ia i nā manu e kīkaha ana ma ka makani. Ke hiamoe nei ke keiki kāne li'ili'i. Ua māluhiluhi loa 'o ia.

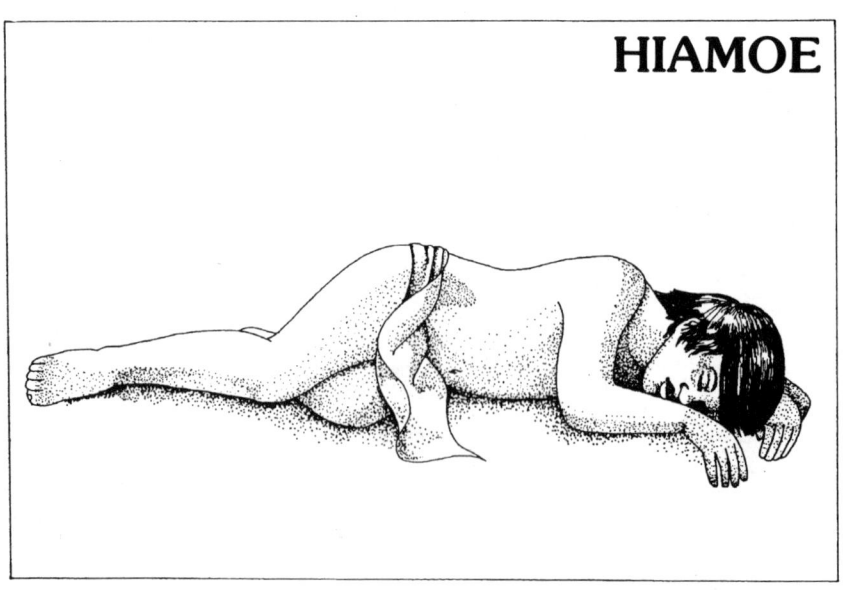

HANA

He mea koʻikoʻi ka hana i ka wā kahiko. Ua hana nā kāne i ka loʻi kalo. Ma hope o ka ʻohi ʻana i ke kalo, ua hoʻomoʻa ʻia. A laila, na ke kāne i kuʻi i ka paʻiʻai no ka hana ʻana i ka poi. Na ka wahine i kuku i ka wauke no ka hana ʻana i ke kapa. He mau hana nui kēia.

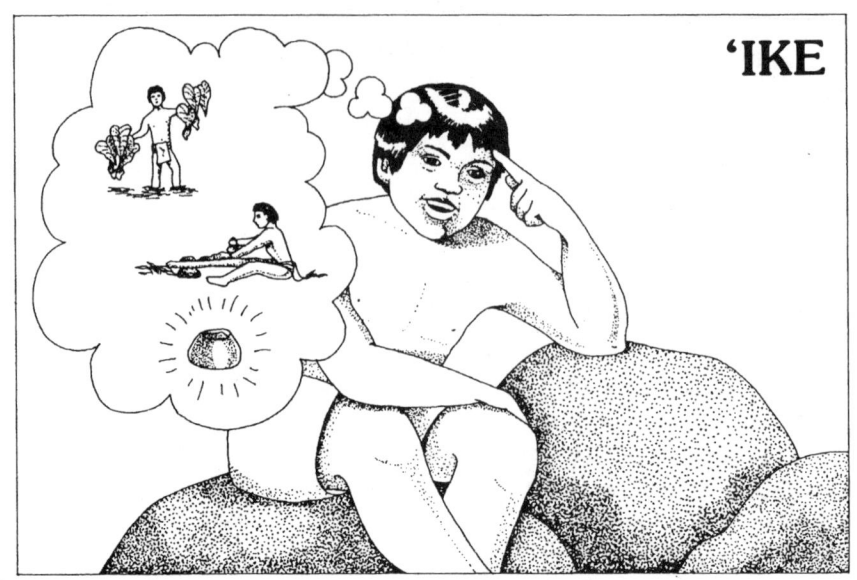

'Ike ke keiki kāne i ka lo'i kalo a mana'o 'o ia i ka poi. Pōloli 'o ia. 'Ike 'o ia i ka hana 'ana i ka poi no ka mea, kōkua 'o ia i kona makua kāne. Ke nānā aku nei ke kaikamahine i nā keiki e pā'ani ana i kahakai. Ua 'ōlelo kona makuahine, "E nānā pono 'oe i kou mau kaikaina!"

'ŌLELO

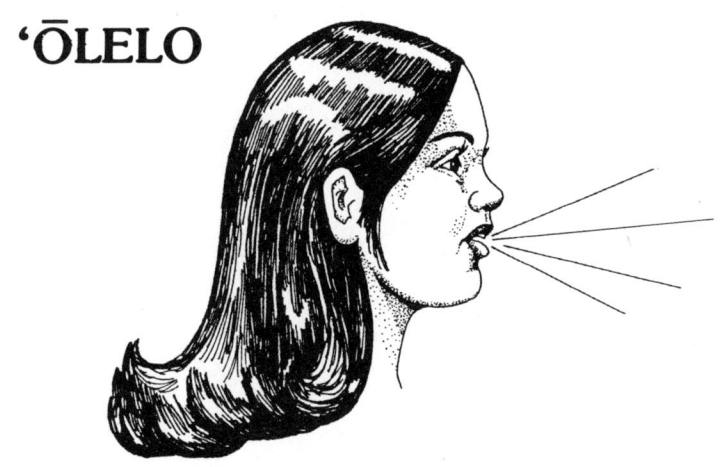

'Ōlelo ka wahine i ka 'ōlelo Hawai'i. Ke 'ōlelo aku nei 'o ia i kāna keiki. Ho'olohe ke keiki i kona makuahine. Ua hana kolohe paha ke keiki a huhū ka makuahine. Hau'oli ke keiki 'ē a'e no ka mea, lohe 'o ia i ka mele nani.

HO'OLOHE

LOHE

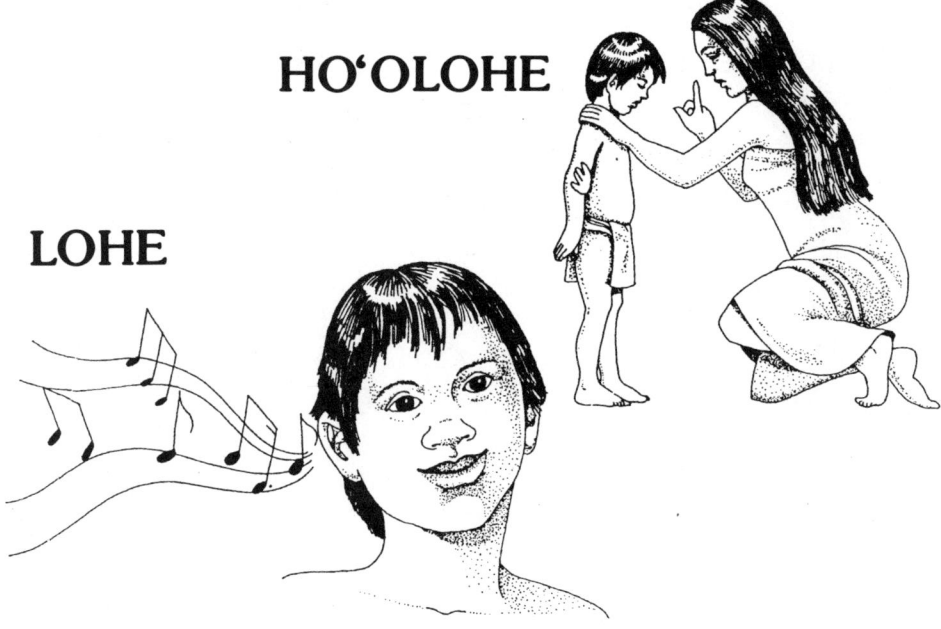

HELU

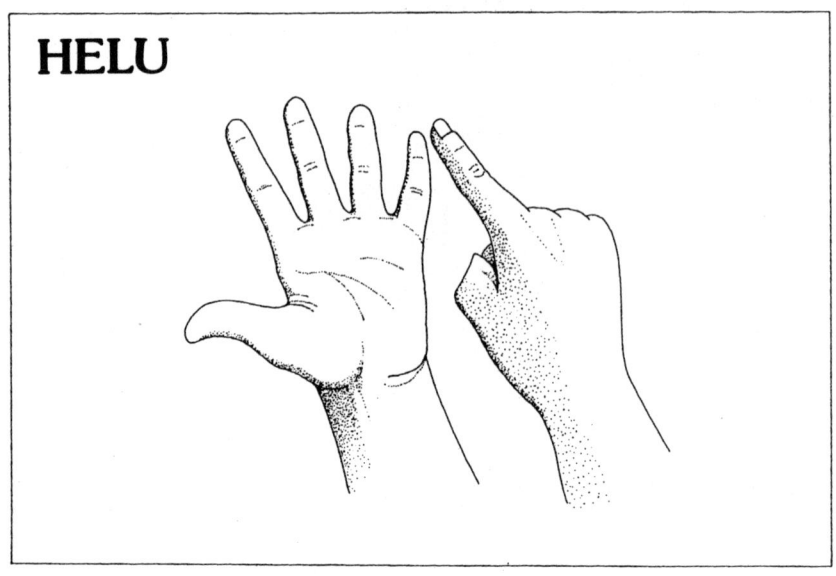

E helu kākou mai ʻekahi a hiki i ʻelima:
  1 ʻekahi
  2 ʻelua
  3 ʻekolu
  4 ʻehā
  5 ʻelima

Hiki iā ʻoukou ke helu ma nā manamana lima.
E hoʻomau i ka helu ʻana a hiki i ʻumi:
  6 ʻeono
  7 ʻehiku
  8 ʻewalu
  9 ʻeiwa
  10 ʻumi

Maikaʻi! Ua akamai ʻoukou i ka helu ʻana ma ka ʻōlelo Hawaiʻi!

Ke hele mai nei ka hoaaloha o Kekoa. E pāʻani pū ana lāua i kēia lā. Ke pau ka pāʻani ʻana, hele aku ka hoaaloha a hoʻi i kona hale. Eia kekahi mau pāʻani a nā keiki—holo kekahi keiki kāne ma ka mauʻu a lele kekahi keiki kāne ʻē aʻe i luna o nā pōhaku.

HULA

He ʻōlapa kēia.
Ke hula nei ʻo ia.
Ua lei ʻo ia i ka lei poʻo a me ka lei ʻāʻī.
Aia nā kūpeʻe i kona mau lima a me kona mau wāwae.

LŌʻIHI

PŌKOLE

Ke kū nei lāua i luna. ʻO ka makua kāne, he kanaka lōʻihi ʻo ia. ʻO kāna kaikamahine, ʻano pōkole ʻo ia. Ke nānā aku nei lāua i ka makuahine e noho ana ma ka mauʻu. Aia ka ʻumeke ma kona ʻaoʻao hema. Ua mākaukau paha ka meaʻai. Ke kali nei ka wahine i kāna kāne a me kāna kaikamahine. E noho pū ana lākou a pau i lalo a ʻai.

NOHO

Ua hauʻoli kēia makuahine no ka mea, he pāʻū hou ko kāna kaikamahine. Ua nani ka lole a ua hauʻoli loa ke kaikamahine i kona pāʻū hou. Ua kaumaha ka makuahine ʻē aʻe no ka mea, he pāʻū kahiko wale nō ko kāna kaikamahine.

NANI

Ua nani kēia kaikamahine. Ua lei ʻo ia i ka lei pua a ua kau ʻo ia i ka pua ma kona pepeiao ʻākau. Ke kali paha nei ʻo ia i kāna ipo. Eia ʻo ia ma lalo nei. He kanaka uʻi ʻo ia. Ua hauʻoli loa kēia kāne uʻi i ka nani o kāna ipo wahine.

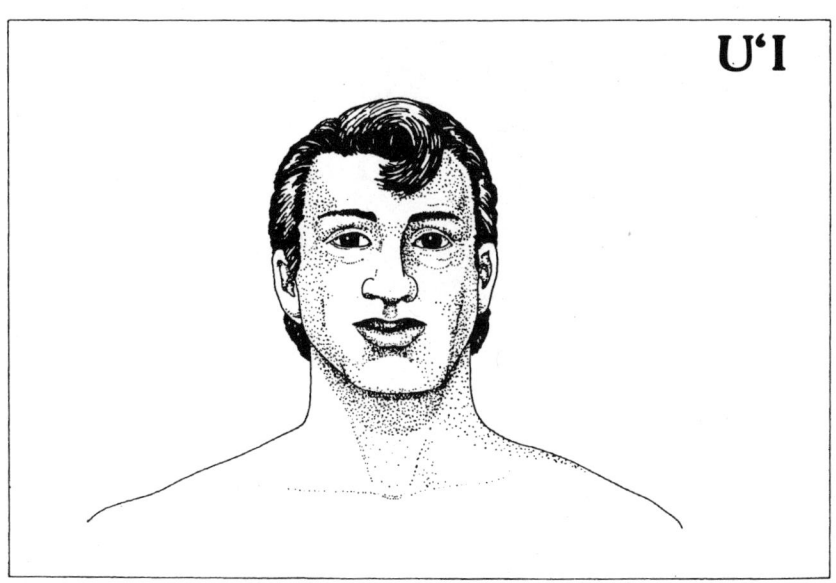

UʻI

Eia 'elua wāhine. Ua 'oko'a loa ko lāua mau 'ano. 'O ka wahine i luna a'e nei, ua momona kona kino. 'Ai loa paha 'o ia. I ka wā ma mua, ua like ka hapanui o nā ali'i wāhine i kona 'ano. 'O ka wahine ma lalo iho nei, ua wīwī loa 'o ia. 'O ia paha ke 'ano o nā wāhine maka'āinana no ka mea, ua hana nui lākou a 'a'ohe nui ka mea'ai kōhi na lākou.

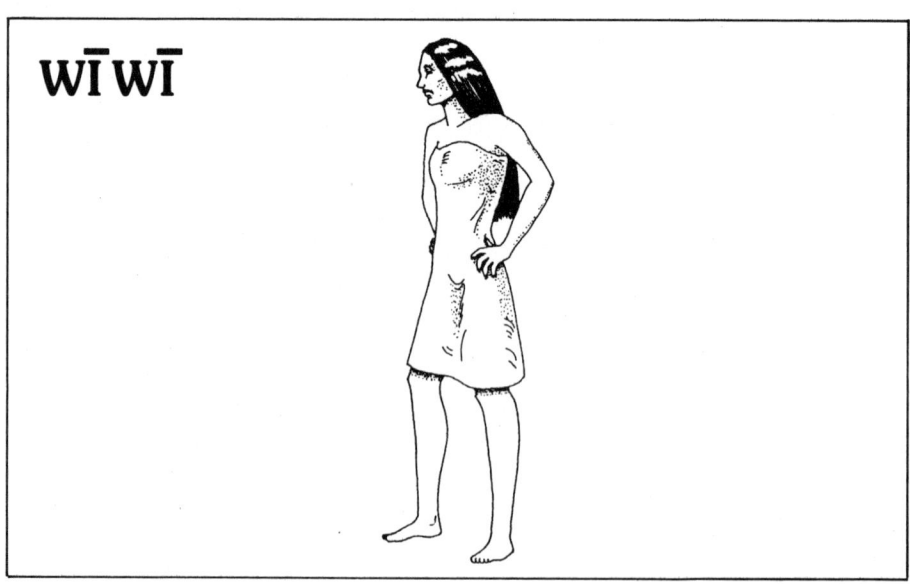

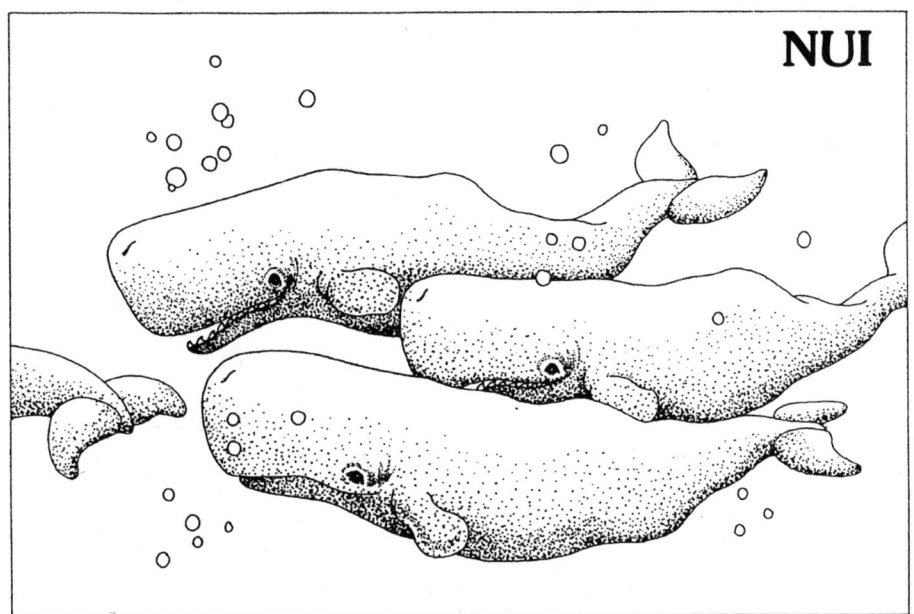
NUI

He mau iʻa kēia. He nui nā ʻano iʻa i loko o ke kai. ʻO nā palaoa he mau iʻa nui. ʻO nā iʻa i lalo, he mau iʻa liʻiliʻi. ʻO kekahi he iʻa ʻuʻuku no ka mea, he iʻa liʻiliʻi loa.

LIʻILIʻI

ʻUʻUKU

He lā wela kēia. Hou nui ke keiki kāne. No ka wela nui o ka lā, makemake ke keiki kāne e ʻauʻau i ka loko wai. Aia kona kaikuahine e ʻauʻau ana i ke kai. Makemake ʻoe e ʻauʻau kai?

ANUANU

Ua anuanu kēia keiki kāne no ka mea, he lā makani a anuanu kēia. 'A'ohe ona kīhei no laila, ke kū'ululū nei 'o ia no ke anu. He nui ka makani i kēia lā. E nānā i ka holu nape a ka lau o ka niu.

E nānā i ke kai. He lā mālie kēia. ʻAʻohe nalu, ʻaʻohe makani a ʻaʻohe ua i kēia lā mālie. Akā, i ke kiʻi ma lalo, he lā ʻino ia. He nui ka makani a he nui nā nalu ma ke kai.

LOLE
Clothing

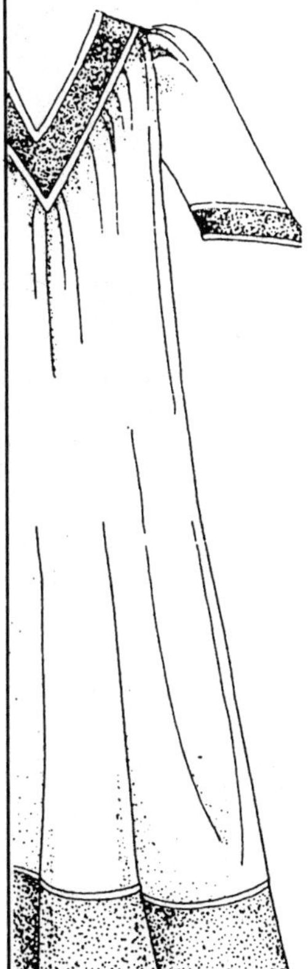

kāmaʻa
malo
muʻumuʻu
pāpale
pāʻū

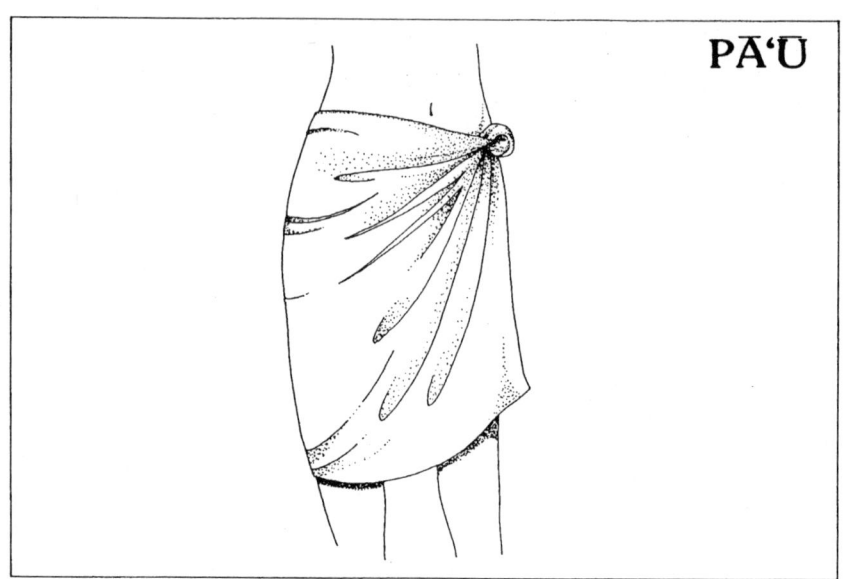

PĀʻŪ

Eia nā ʻano o ka lole Hawaiʻi i ka wā kahiko. Komo nā wāhine i ka pāʻū. Ua like ka pāʻū me ka pareu Tahiti a i ʻole ka lavalava Kāmoa. Hume nā kāne i ka malo. ʻO ka malo he ʻāpana kapa ia.

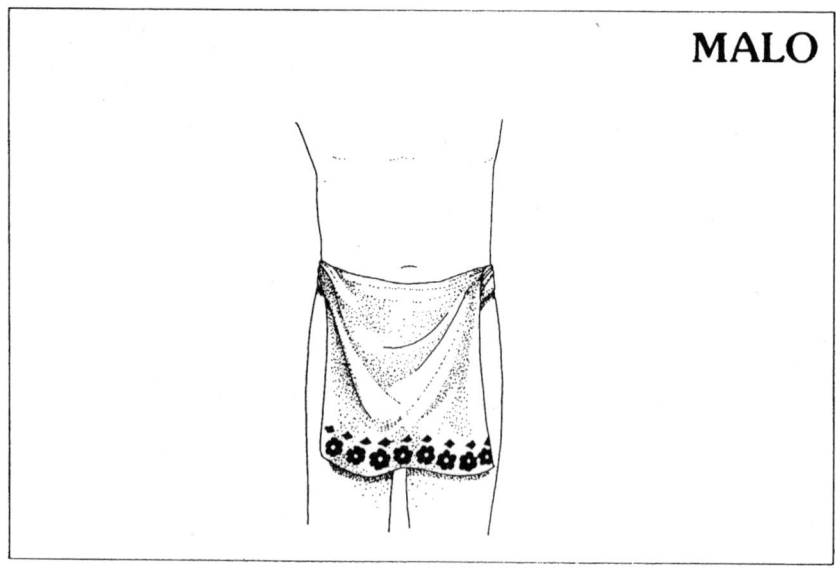

MALO

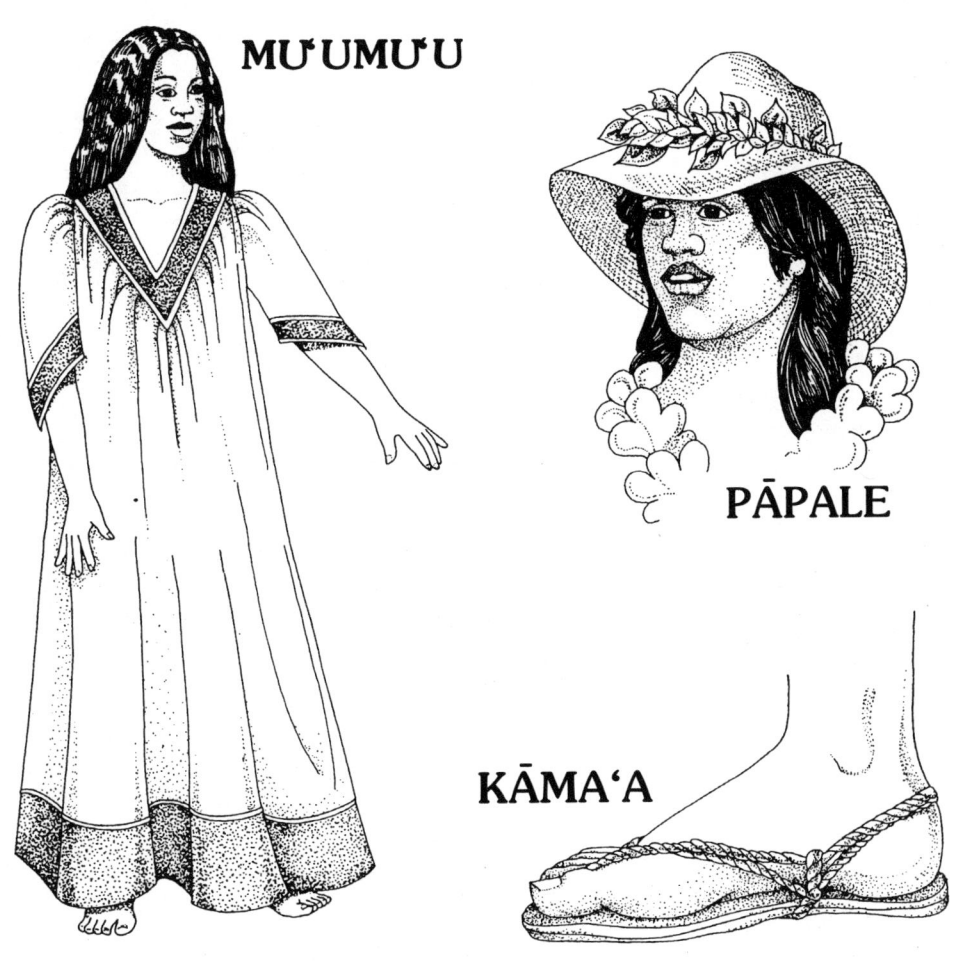

Eia kekahi mau ʻano lole. Ua komo ka wahine i ka muʻumuʻu. Aia ka pāpale ma ke poʻo o ke kaikamahine. He lei kona ma luna o ka pāpale. Aia ka wāwae i loko o ke kāmaʻa.

AIA I HEA?
Relative Locations

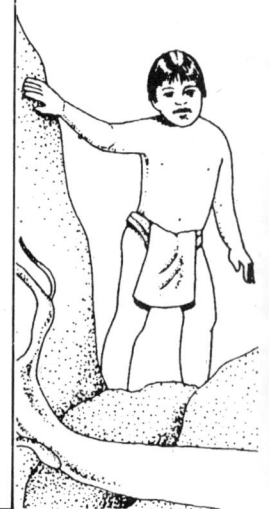

hope
kokoke
lalo
loko
luna
ma kai

mamao
ma uka
mua
waena
waho

Aia kekahi ʻīlio e pāʻani nei ma waho o ka hīnaʻi.
Ke māluhiluhi ʻo ia, ua piʻi ʻo ia i loko o ka hīnaʻi a kiaʻi i nā mea a pau o waho.
Aia ke kaikamahine e noho nei ma luna o ka haka.
Ke ua mai, hiki iā ia ke noho i lalo o ka haka.

E hele ana nā keiki i ka mākaʻikaʻi ʻana. Aia kekahi keiki kāne ma mua o lākou. Hahai kona kaikuahine a me kona kaikuaʻana iā ia. Aia kekahi kaikamahine i waena o lākou. He pua kona ma ka lauoho. Aia kekahi keiki kāne ʻē aʻe ma hope o lākou. Ua lohi ʻo ia.

I ka wā ma mua, ua noho ka hapanui o ka poʻe Hawaiʻi i nā wahi ma kai. Ua hiki iā lākou ke lawaiʻa. Ua kokoke nā kauhale i nā loʻi kalo ma nā ʻāina kula. I kekahi manawa, ua hele ka poʻe i nā wahi ma uka no ka ʻohi ʻana i nā huaʻai a me ka wahie. Ua mamao nā wahi uka mai ke kahakai.

MA KE KULA
At School

kini ʻōpala	palapala ʻāina	poho
mea holoi	papaʻeleʻele	puka
kiʻi	peni	pukaaniani
noho	penikala	puke
pākaukau	pepa	uaki

He kula kēia. Hele nā haumāna i ke kula
no ka 'imi na'auao 'ana. A'o mai lākou i nā mea
he nui. 'O ka heluhelu 'ana a me ke kākau 'ana
nā mea ko'iko'i loa. A'o aku nā kumu kula
i nā kumuhana like 'ole i nā haumāna. I kekahi o
nā kula, a'o aku nā kūpuna i ka 'ōlelo a me
nā mea Hawai'i 'ē a'e.

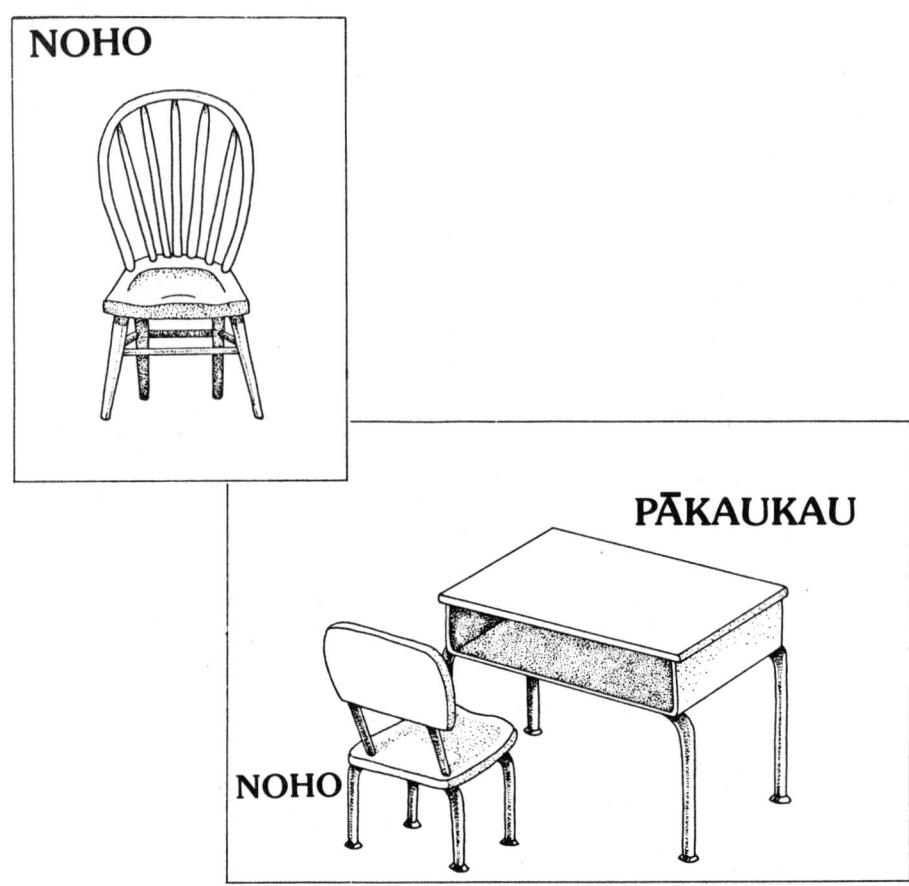

Eia 'elua 'ano noho. I ka wā ma mua, ua noho ka po'e Hawai'i ma luna o ka moena, 'a'ole ma ka noho. He mea ia i lawe 'ia mai e ka po'e Haole. Aia ka noho kula ma hope o ka pākaukau hana. Noho ka haumāna i luna o kēlā 'ano noho i loko o ka lumi kula.

PENIKALA

PEPA

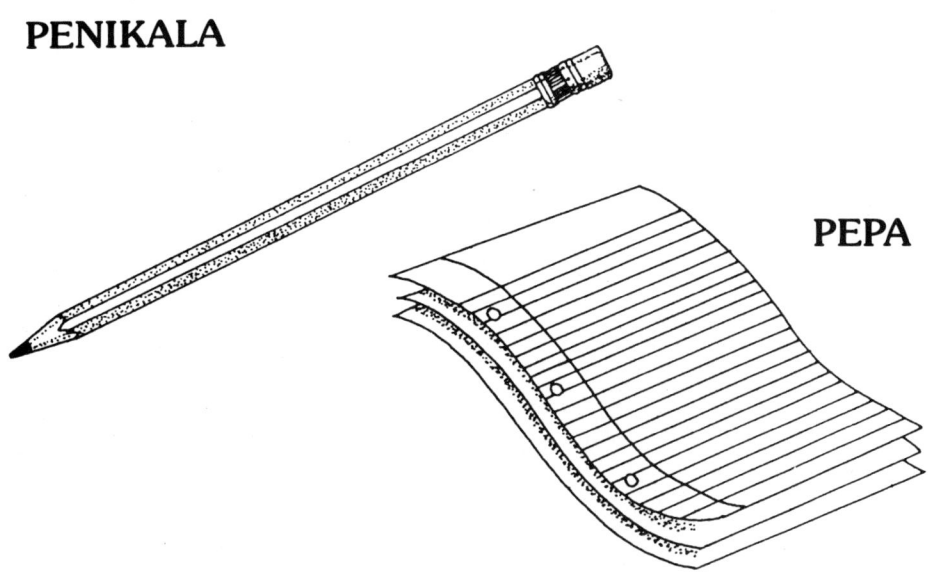

Eia kekahi mau mea no ke kākau ʻana. Hiki iā ʻoe ke kākau ma luna o ka pepa me ka peni a i ʻole me ka penikala. Inā he hewa kou i ke kākau ʻana, hoʻoponopono ʻoe i ka hewa me ka mea holoi a e kākau hou i ka mea pololei.

PENI

MEA HOLOI

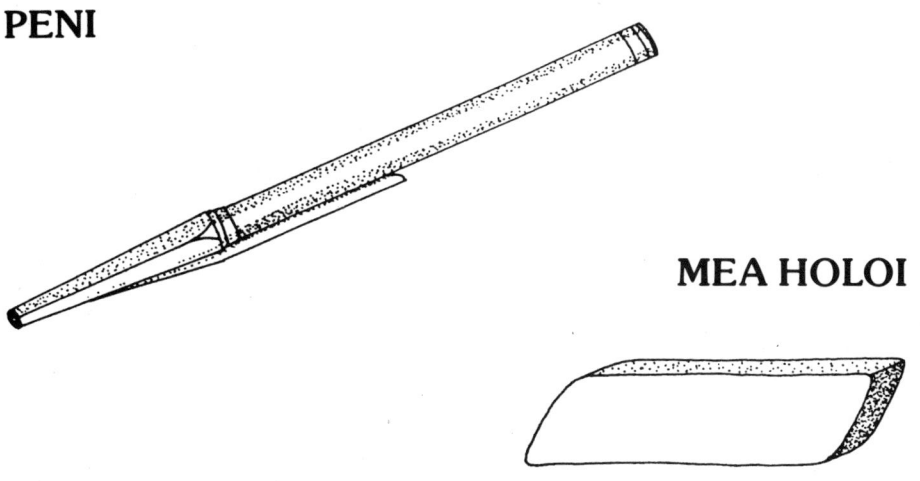

POHO

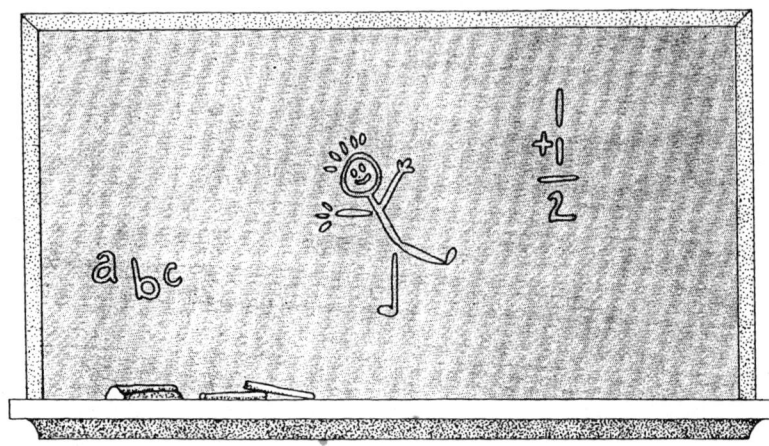

PAPAʻELEʻELE

Eia kekahi mau mea kūpono no ka lumi kula. Kākau ke kumu a i ʻole nā haumāna ma ka papaʻeleʻele me ka poho. Kau nā kiʻi a me nā palapala ʻāina ma ka paia o ka lumi kula. ʻO kēia he kiʻi o ke kumulāʻau.

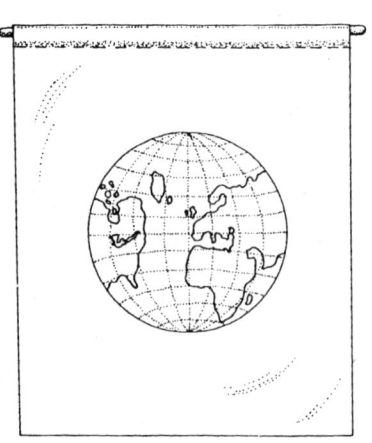

PALAPALA ʻĀINA

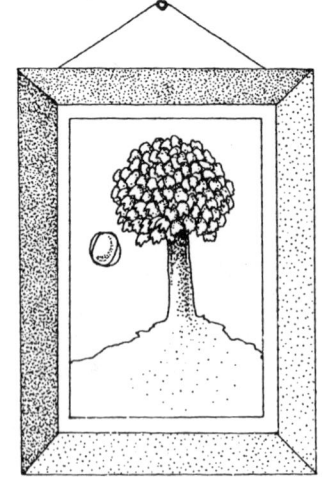

KIʻI

PUKE

Eia kekahi mau mea 'ē a'e no ka lumi kula. 'O ka puke he mea ko'iko'i no ke a'o 'ana mai. I ka manawa o nā mikionali, ua makemake loa ka po'e Hawai'i e a'o mai i ka heluhelu 'ana. He mea nui 'o ka uaki no ka 'ike 'ana i ka manawa pololei. Aia ka uaki ma ka paia o ka lumi kula. Pono nā haumāna e kiloi i ka 'ōpala i loko o ke kini 'ōpala.

UAKI

KINI 'ŌPALA

English Translations of the Hawaiian Sentences

The following translations are meant to be rather literal renderings instead of polished English colloquial phrases so that students of the Hawaiian language may better understand the structure and composition of the various Hawaiian sentence patterns. The page number given before each set of sentence translations corresponds to the page on which the drawing(s) and sentences can be found.

1 - Ko ka poʻe kānaka. About people.
2 - This is a wooden image. This is a god image/statue. This statue is a symbol of the god, Kū. In the old days, the statue was a symbol of the power of the gods.
3 - These are chiefly persons. The male chief is clad in a cloak. The feathered helmet is on his head. He is wearing a loincloth. There is a fan in the right hand of the chiefess. She is wearing the sperm whale tooth pendant. A feather garland is placed on the head.
4 - This is a priestly expert. He has strong spiritual power. There were many kinds of experts in the old days.
5 - These are commoners. The man is a cultivator perhaps. There is a digging stick in his right hand. He is dressed in a loincloth. The woman is sitting down. She is dressed in a wrap-around garment. Her hair is long. She is a beautiful woman.
6 - These are outcasts. They (2) were perhaps captured in a war. They were tattooed with brands on the face. That was a sign of their status.
7 - Names are the subject of this drawing. Kekoa is the name of the boy. Kuʻulei and Mokihana are the names of the girls. What is your name? What is the name of the dog?
8 - This is a person/human being. He is alone. He is standing with a spear in the right hand. He is dressed in a loincloth.
9 - These are people/human beings. In the drawing, there are four men, two women, four boys and one girl. These people are Hawaiians.
10 - This is a man. He is dressed in a loincloth. The arms are folded. Perhaps he is a chief's agent.
11 - These are men. They are having a discussion in the shade of the coconut tree.
12 - This is a woman. She is dressed in a wrap-around garment with a shawl on the left shoulder. This woman is beautiful with her long hair.

13 - These are women. Two of them are standing up. Three of them are sitting down. They are gathered in front of the house.
14 - The garland is the subject of this drawing. The woman is putting a garland of *Alyxia olivaeformis* on the man. There is a head wreath on the head of the woman. That is a flower wreath. The woman greets the man. The man thanks the woman.
15 - This is a Hawaiian family. This is a genealogy. There are four grandparents, the mother and her brother, the father and his sister and four children. There are two daughters, one son, and one infant boy in this family.
16 - This is a grandparent/elder. She is a grandmother. She is standing with her grandson. She is dressed in a wrap-around garment with a shawl on the left shoulder. The boy is happy.
17 - These are grandparents/elders. The grandmother and the grandfather are sitting in the shade of the coconut trees. The grandfather is an old man. The grandmother is an old woman. Perhaps they (2) are resting.
18 - This is a parent. He is a father. He is carrying his infant on his left arm. The father loves his child.
19 - These are parents. There are three fathers and two mothers in the drawing. The father is standing with his younger brother and his cousin. The mother is beating barkcloth. She is sitting down with her older sister.
20 - These are children. There is one girl, one boy and one infant in the picture. The children are standing up. The baby is sitting down in the grass. The native hibiscus flower is placed on the right ear of the girl.
21 - This is a grass house. In the early times, the Hawaiian people lived in housing compounds. There was a building appropriate for each activity. Here are some types of buildings: the men's eating house/family shrine, the women and children's eating house, the free-from-taboo sleeping house, the cooking house, the menstrual house, the barkcloth beating house, and so forth. The house was built on a stone foundation. There still are house foundations from the old days in various places existing today.
22 - These pictures have some kinds of perforations. In the old days, the people entered the house through the hole (in the wall). It was a true hole in the wall of the house. In these times, there is a wooden door or a glass door for closing the hole of the house. The tree does not have a perforation; the correct word is a hollow. You can see through the window of a house.
23 - This is a mat and a pillow. Hawaiian women were skillful in plaiting mats. They plaited mats for the house, pandanus leaf pillows, fans, bags, and so forth. This pillow is a new type of pillow. It is not made of pandanus leaf, but is made from cloth and feathers. In earlier times, the Hawaiian people slept on pandanus mats, but now we all sleep in a bed.

24 - Here are two kinds of chairs. In former times, Hawaiians sat on mats, not on chairs. It's a thing brought by the foreigner. There is a school chair behind the desk. The students sit on that kind of chair in the school room.

25 - The Body

26 - This is the human body. The head is on top of the body. This is a boy. He has one head. He has two arms. He has two legs.

27 - This is the human body. There are some of the parts of the body. How many eyes does he have? He has two eyes. How many mouths does he have? He has one mouth. He has two ears. He has one nose. How many fingers does he have? He has ten fingers. How many toes does he have? He has ten toes.

28 - These are some parts of the inside of the human body. There is the back in back of the body. There is the heart above the stomach. There are the intestines below the stomach. There are many bones in the human body.

29 - Hawaiian Lifestyle.

30 - This is the day. The sun shines during the day. There is the sun in the sky above the house and the coconut trees.

31 - This is the night. The moon and the stars shine at night.

32 - The girl awakes in the morning. She is stretching her arms. She is yawning because she is still sleepy.

33 - The boy rests in the midday. He is climbing the coconut tree. He is seeking the refreshing water of the coconut.

34 - The fisherman prepares his net in the afternoon. Maybe he wants to go fishing.

35 - The sun sets in the evening. These lovers are watching the setting of the sun.

36 - This is a rainbow. There is the rainbow in the sky. The rainbow arches when fine rain falls in the daytime. The fisherman is happy to see the rain. He thinks, "It's raining, life up in the plains will continue." Rain is a very good thing for taro.

37 - This is the wind. (When) the wind blows, it's a stormy day. With one fast sweep of wind, all is gone. The wind blows, the sea is white with foam.

38 - This is a mountain spewing forth lava. There are volcanoes in Hawai'i and in other lands on this earth. The Hawaiian people thought, Pele is the goddess of the volcano. She is the one who enlarges the land of Puna with the lava flowing to the sea.

39 - This is fire. Maui gave fire to humans in the very early days. People could cook food. Fire is a blessing sometimes and a bad thing at other times. Children should take care with fire or the house can be destroyed by fire!

40 - There are ridge-backed mountains on the older islands, that is, Kaua'i and O'ahu. There are shield-shaped mountains on the somewhat younger islands such as Maui and Hawai'i. All of the islands have waterfalls. The waterfalls on the windward side of Moloka'i are exceedingly beautiful! The water of the stream flows over the large and small rocks.

41 - There are birds soaring on the constant wind of the windward cliffs of the different islands. These cliffs are high. There are trees growing on top of the cliffs. There is also the *Phymatosorus scolopendria* fern growing beneath the trees.

42 - This is a leaf in the top picture. (It's) the leaf of the plumeria perhaps. That plant was brought from Central America. There are many kinds of different flowers on the trees in Hawai'i. The majority of the flowers are beautiful and fragrant. One can make various garlands with the flowers. There are three types of vegetation in the picture. The big tree may be a mango tree. The fruit of this tree is very delicious.

43 - This is a hand of bananas. In the old days, there were many varieties of banana. The ripe fruit of the banana is yellow.

44 - These are coconut trees with the nuts. This is a riddle about the coconut: Three enclosures and you'll reach the water. That is, the husk, the shell and the coconut meat.

45 - The boy is drinking coconut water. Coconut water is delicious on hot days.

46 - The girl is eating *poi*. *Poi* is truly delicious to the Hawaiians. *Poi* was the most important food for the Hawaiian people.

47 - This is *taro*. *Taro* was the most important plant to the Hawaiians. They pounded the cooked *taro* for hard, mashed *taro*. When you mix water into the hard, mashed *taro*, you get *poi*. *Poi* is really delicious with fish.

48 - The girl is walking along the path. Perhaps she is bringing food to her brothers. They(2) are working in the food garden. Their bodies are dirty. One of the boys holds a *taro* in his left hand. Sweet potato grows in a dirt mound.

49 - These are breadfruit. Hawaiians ate breadfruit. Samoans and Tongans like breadfruit very much.

50 - This is sweet potato. (This was) also a very important plant for the Hawaiians. This is a bodily manifestation of the god Lono.

51 - This is sugarcane. Sugarcane grew in the old times in Hawai'i. There are many new varieties growing today.

52 - This is a pig. The Polynesians brought the pig to Hawai'i. The pig is steambaked in the underground oven. We all eat steambaked pork at a party or a feast.

53 - This is a dog. Hawaiians raised dogs for eating. The type of Hawaiian dog was a "*poi* dog."

54 - This is a chicken. It is a rooster with a beautiful tail.

55 - This is a papaya. *Mīkana* is another name for this plant. This fruit is delicious for breakfast.

56 - This is a pineapple. (It's) an important plant for this era. Some people think that the Hawaiians had the *halakea* (white pineapple) and the *halaʻula* (reddish pineapple) in the early days.

57 - This is the passion fruit. You can make truly delicious juice with the fruits.

58 - There is the beach on the edge of the sea. Hawaiians frequently go to the beach. We like to camp there. The children can play on the sand. The parents can fish in the sea. Most of the people like to sea bathe/swim in the ocean.

59 - There are three people aboard the single-hulled canoe. There they are paddling on the ocean. Perhaps they are fishermen. They are going to paddle the canoe to the deep sea. Look at the characteristics of the Hawaiian paddle.

60 - This is a big wave. The Hawaiians like very much to surf on various kinds of waves.

61 - This is a surfboard. This boy is skilled at surfing. He surfs the big waves. The *alaia* (short board) is the type of his surfboard. The short board was made of breadfruit, *Acacia koa* and *Erythrina sandwicensis* in the old days.

62 - This is seaweed. This is an important food from the sea. There are many kinds of seaweed.

63 - These are fish. Fish was an important food for the common people in the old days. Fish is a food that's appropriate for good health. There are many kinds of fish in the "eight seas of Hawaiʻi" (the seas surrounding the eight major islands of Hawaiʻi).

64 - These are shells. The eight seas of Hawaiʻi have many kinds of shells. The shell garland is the garland of Niʻihau.

65 - Verbs and Adjectives

66 - The girl is standing up. Her brother is reclining/lying down under the coconut tree. He is looking at the birds soaring on the wind. The little boy is sleeping. He is very tired.

67 - Work was very important in the old days. The men worked in the *taro* patch. After harvesting the *taro*, it was cooked. Then it was the man who pounded it to hard, mashed *taro* for making *poi*. It was the woman who beat the indian mulberry for making barkcloth. These were very important activities.

68 - The boy sees the *taro* patch and he thinks of *poi*. He is hungry. He knows how to make *poi* because he helps his father. The girl is looking at the children playing at the beach. Her mother said, "Look carefully after your younger sisters!"

69 - The woman speaks the Hawaiian language. She is speaking to her child. The child listens to his mother. Maybe the child did something naughty and the mother is angry. The other child is happy because he is listening to a beautiful song.

70 - Let's all count from one to five: one, two, three, four, five. You can count on the fingers. Continue counting to ten: six, seven, eight, nine, ten. Good! You all are smart at counting in the Hawaiian language!

71 - The friend of Kekoa is coming. They two will play together today. When the playing is finished, the friend goes and returns to his house. Here are some of the children's games – one boy runs on the grass and the other boy jumps over the rocks.

72 - This is a dancer (of ancient dance). She is dancing. She is garlanded with a head garland and a necklace. There are bracelets on her arms and anklets on her legs.

73 - They two are standing up. The father, he is a tall man. His daughter, she is kind of short. They two are looking at the mother sitting on the grass. There is a calabash on her left side. Maybe the food is ready. The woman is waiting for her husband and her daughter. They will all sit down together and eat.

74 - This mother is happy because her daughter has a new wrap-around garment. The other mother is sad because her daughter only has an old wrap-around garment.

75 - This girl is pretty. She is garlanded in a flower garland and she has placed a flower on her right ear. Perhaps she is waiting for her sweetheart. Here he is below. He is a handsome man. This good-looking man is very happy about the beauty of his girlfriend.

76 - Here are two women. Their characteristics are very different. The woman up above, her body is fat. Perhaps she eats a lot. In the early days, most of the chiefesses were like her type. The woman below here, she is very thin. That is perhaps the characteristic of commoner women because they worked a lot and there was not much rich, fatty food for them.

77 - These are sea animals. There are many kinds of fish in the sea. Sperm whales are large sea creatures. The fishes below are little fishes. One (of them) is a tiny fish because (it is) a very small fish.

78 - This is a hot day. The boy is sweating a lot. Because of the great heat of the sun, the boy wants to swim in the fresh water pool. There is his sister swimming in the ocean. Do you like to sea bathe?

79 - This boy is cold because this is a windy and cold day. He does not have a shawl, therefore he is shivering because of the cold. There is a lot of wind today. Look at the swaying of the coconut fronds.

80 - Look at the ocean. This is a calm day. (There are) no waves, no wind and no rain on this calm day. But, in the picture below, it's a stormy day. (There are) a lot of wind and a lot of waves in the sea.

81 - Clothing
82 - Here are the kinds of Hawaiian clothing in the old days. The women wore a wrap-around garment. The *pāʻū* is like the Tahitian *pareu* or the Samoan *lavalava.* Men wore the loincloth. The *malo* is a piece of barkcloth.
83 - Here are some kinds of clothing. The woman is dressed in a *muʻumuʻu.* The hat is on the head of the girl. She has a garland on the hat. The foot is in the shoe/footwear.
84 - Relative locations
85 - There is a dog playing outside of the basket. When it tires, it climbs inside of the basket and watches everything outside. The girl is sitting on top of the platform. When it rains, she can sit under the platform.
86 - The children are going sightseeing. There is one boy in front of them. His sister and his older brother follow him. There is a girl in the middle of them. She has a flower in her hair. There is another boy behind them. He is slow.
87 - In the early days, most of the Hawaiian people lived in areas by the sea. They were able to fish. The housing compounds were close to the *taro* patches in the midland areas. Sometimes, the people went to the upland areas for the gathering of fruit and firewood. The upland areas are far from the seashore.
88 - At School
89 - This is a school. The students go to school to seek knowledge. They learn many things. Reading and writing are the most important things. The school teachers teach the various subjects to the students. In some schools, elders teach the Hawaiian language and other Hawaiian things.
90 - Here are two kinds of chairs. In the early days, Hawaiians sat on mats, not on chairs. It's something which was brought by the foreigners. There is a school chair behind the desk. The students sit on that kind of chair in the school room.
91 - Here are some things for writing. You can write on the paper with the pen or the pencil. If you have a mistake in writing, you correct the mistake with the eraser and write the correct thing again.
92 - Here are some things appropriate for the school room. The teacher or the students write on the blackboard with chalk. Pictures and maps hang on the wall of the school room. This is a picture of a tree.
93 - Here are some other things for the school room. The book is an important thing for learning. At the time of the missionaries, Hawaiians wanted to learn to read. The clock is an important thing for knowing the correct time. The clock is on the wall of the school room. The students should throw the trash into the rubbish can.